TOM LAWTON'S
SHORT WALKS
IN THE
LAKE DISTRICT

Photographs by the author

WARD LOCK

To those of all ages who enjoy a short walk, be this a leisurely stroll by the side of a lake, an energetic climb to the top of a commanding fell, or a combination of the two.

The walking routes described in this book comply with the guidelines for writers of path guides issued by the Outdoor Writers' Guild.

This edition first published in the UK 2000 for
The Book People Ltd, Hall Wood Avenue, Haydock,
St Helens WA11 9UL

A British Library Cataloguing in Publication Data block for this book may be obtained from the British Library

ISBN 0 7063 7520 3

Typeset by York House Typographic Ltd, London
Printed and bound in Slovenia by Delo-Tiskarna d.d.
by arrangement with Korotan Ljubljana d.o.o.

CONTENTS

PREFACE

IT is generally accepted that walking is one of the healthiest of exercises and, if undertaken regularly, will make a significant contribution to physical fitness. Happily, it is an exercise which may be pursued by young and old alike; by people of all shapes and sizes, and at most starting levels of fitness and physical capability; and by oneself, with friends, in family groups or with larger walking parties. It is fortunate, therefore, that walking is such pleasant recreation, and this is particularly true when the walks pass through areas of outstanding natural beauty – of which there are many in the favoured landscapes of the British Isles. The National Parks were, in fact, designated to preserve this precious natural heritage and to make these areas generally accessible to the public. Since then, walking through these Parks has become an exceptionally popular pastime, generating for the walker not only enjoyment and a feeling of well-being, but also a better understanding of the landscape and a closeness with nature that is often missing in our hectic urban lives. We have also become healthier as we walk!

Elterwater and the Langdale Pikes.

The Lake District National Park in particular has much to offer walkers, especially those keen on short walks. One reason for this is the unique, glaciated topography of the area with placid lakes, tiny tarns, meandering rivers, gushing waterfalls, tranquil woodlands, dense forested areas, sheltered valleys and exposed, craggy fells, all squeezed together by the violent forces of nature to create a compact countryside of endless variation and – in the view of many – unsurpassed magnificence. In addition, there is a multitude of places of interest to be discovered and explored in Lakeland. Brantwood, Dove Cottage, Castlerigg Stone Circle, Fell Foot Park, Mediobognum Roman Fort, Rydal Mount… these are just a few which spring immediately to mind, while a sail on the National Trust steam yacht *Gondola* or a ride on the narrow–gauge Ravenglass & Eskdale Railway are two novel ways of reaching the starting point of your walk.

The selection of short walks in this book includes several very popular, well-known routes, but it also introduces a number of much less frequented trails and paths. This also applies to the places of interest visited. Each walk is described in detail and illustrated with colour photographs and innovative diagrams. My hope is that this collection of walks, and the way in which it is presented, will provide further purpose and inspiration for those who have already trod these ways, as well as an irresistible incentive for others to do so. Should these hopes be realized, my endeavours will have been well rewarded.

Tom Lawton

ACKNOWLEDGEMENTS

GAIN, it gives me pleasure to record my gratitude to the many kind people who have contributed to the completion of another book. They have once more given generously of their precious time and expertise to make this latest walking guide possible. To all of you, please accept my warm appreciation and sincere thanks for your efforts – and for the understanding way you met my deadlines!

My special thanks are due to several friends and walking companions who accompanied me on the walks and/or contributed in other ways. In particular, I would like to thank Chris Sennitt, with his empathy for the Lake District; Eddie Fidler and Bob Carter, who meticulously checked my draft manuscript and audited the proof stages of the book; and Ian Morris, who continued to keep my computer systems upgraded.

May I also express my appreciation to the knowledgeable Rangers of the Lake District National Park for checking through the text of the walking routes, and for their guidance and constructive advice; I am also indebted to Bob Cartwright and Andrew Lovett, who organized this. Additionally, the routes through Grizedale and Whinlatter Forests have been checked by the Forest Rangers, and I am grateful to Paul Burke and his colleagues for showing me the woods from the trees.

I talked to many fellow walkers while out and about, and these exchanges of views and experiences between people who share a common bond once again stimulated my endeavours and gave further purpose and direction to my efforts. Their comments and helpful suggestions are much appreciated and valued.

Finally, may I once again express my thanks and gratitude for their cheerful support to my wife Bridget and two daughters Katrina and Helen, who continue to accept this competitive labour of love.

WALK LOCATIONS

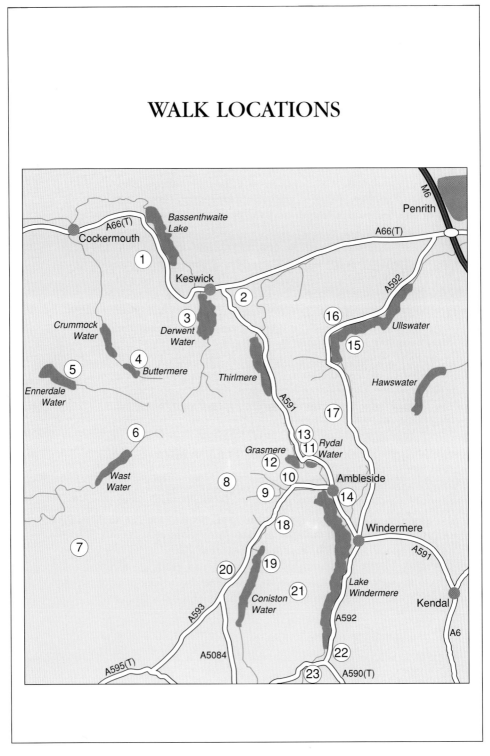

USING THE BOOK

THIS book covers a series of interesting and varied short walks in the beautiful Lake District National Park. These range from easy strolls along sheltered lakesides, involving virtually no climbing at all, to routes that penetrate the lower, open fellsides and may include a relatively energetic and challenging ascent to the summit of a modestly sized mountain or hill. There are numerous places of interest in Lakeland. Wherever possible the walks have been planned to incorporate opportunities for visiting these attractions. In addition, it is possible to reach the starting points of some of the walks via boat trips along several of the larger lakes or by travelling on steam trains. All in all, there should be something for everyone!

THE ROUTES

The route descriptions cover 23 walks in detail and these have been spread over the entire Lake District. In making this selection, a balance has been struck between including 'firm favourites' and introducing some less well-known routes, in the hope that they will become 'new friends'.

All the 'explorations' start from a conveniently located carpark or layby, where possible at a place of interest, and details of these and of other useful facilities available there, such as toilets, picnic areas and information centres, are provided. The route descriptions start from these carparking facilities or, where appropriate, from the embarkation points for the relevant boat or train.

The description of each walk covers the entire route in detail, pointing out features of interest, as well as any possible hazards, along the way and giving careful advice at points where route finding may be less than straightforward. Maps and diagrams are provided for each walk, along with superb colour photographs giving just a taste of the landscapes you will encounter.

WALK DETAILS

Each route description begins with an information summary which will help you to decide on the suitability of the particular walk for you and your party. The main points are themselves summarized in the table on page 190, to provide an at-a-glance reference to all 23 routes.

GRADING OF WALKS

The time of year, weather and ground conditions on the day, the walker's age, physical condition, walking ability and experience, and his/her knowledge of the area will all affect an individual's appraisal of how difficult they and/or their party may find a particular walking route. Nevertheless, and bearing in mind that all the routes are considered 'short', the walks have been graded as either 'easy/straightforward' or 'moderate/challenging'.

Easy/straightforward These walks are for the most part along fairly level ground, with no sustained, severe or difficult uphill slopes. Where modest climbs are involved, these are well spaced out and not unduly strenuous. There is no potentially dangerous exposure or difficult terrain of any consequence, and the walk covers the minimum of waterlogged ground and few boggy areas. Route finding presents limited problems on these walks and the way is adequately signed. Paths are mostly clear and good, and the greater part of the route is along these. The walk is frequently suitable for family groups with, more often than not, plenty of general interest in addition to the surrounding views and landscapes.

Moderate/challenging These walks remain suitable for all reasonably fit walkers who wish to follow a route which could occupy a good half to full day spent among the fells. However, they do include a combination of features which makes them more exacting than the other category; perhaps some sustained or energetic climbing, together with a longer, more complicated route, sections of which are not as clearly defined as might be expected. On occasion these routes will not be confined to clearly defined footpaths but will involve some walking across the uncharted, open fellsides to provide a taste of more adventurous fell wandering.

This category of walks is less suitable for younger children but should appeal to stronger, older, adventurous youngsters accompanied by experienced adults.

TIME ALLOWANCE

Estimates of walking time have been provided for each route, excluding any allowances for stops such as coffee breaks, lunch and taking photographs. The estimates are generous and have been calculated by allowing 1 hour to walk each 3.2km (2 miles), and a further half an hour for each 250m (750ft) climbed, and a final adjustment of plus or minus half an hour per walk, depending upon additional factors such as ease or difficulty of route finding, state of the paths, type of terrain and so on. You can adjust these basic estimates to suit your own walking speed.

TACKLING THE WALK

Following the summary information at the start of each route description, advice is provided on the appeal and/or adaptability of the walk for three categories: casual walkers, family walkers and dedicated fell walkers. Family walkers will certainly know who they are and, although there may be some overlap between the other two at the borderline, it should be fairly easy to place yourself and/or your party in the relevant category. Read the advice given for each walk to help you decide on its suitability for your purposes, particularly as regards the age and abilities of children who will be able to tackle the route comfortably.

PLACES AND ACTVITIES OF INTEREST

At the end of each route description the main places of interest and other useful information, such as boat trips and train services, are covered in more detail, together with a reference to contact numbers and addresses in the Useful Addresses section.

ABBREVIATIONS

The minimum number of abbreviations has been used in the route descriptions, and only to avoid constant repetition.

L   left
R   right

N	north	m	metre(s)
NNE	north north east	ft	foot/feet
NE	north east	yd	yard(s)
ENE	east north east	km	kilometre(s)
E	east		
ESE	east south east	G-stile	gap stile (squeezer stile)
SE	south east		
SSE	south south east	L-stile	ladder stile
S	south	P-stile	post stile
SSW	south south west	S-stile	step stile
SW	south west	W-stile	wall stile
WSW	west south west	K-gate	kissing gate
W	west	MR	map reference
WNW	west north west	OLM(s)	Outdoor Leisure Map(s)
NW	north west		
NNW	north north west	OS	Ordnance Survey

THE DIAGRAMS

The book contains a diagram for each route, which gives both a plan and a cross-sectional relief of the walk. These diagrams have been computer-generated and are based upon grid reference points taken from Ordnance Survey maps. I have used the Outdoor Leisure series 1:25000; 4 cm to 1 km (2 in to 1 mile). The relief cross-section is mathematically integral with the plan and accurately follows the exact line of the route.

Camera symbols show the position and direction of each photograph taken. These have been allocated a distinctive number identical to that given in the relevant photograph caption. The first part of the number indicates the route, while the second part refers to the sequence of the photograph within each route. Photographs taken on the route are shown by the camera symbol pointing either along or away from the line of the walk, whereas photographs taken of the route from other locations are identified by the camera symbol pointing inwards towards the line of the route.

MAPS AND MISCELLANEOUS

In addition to the maps and route descriptions provided in this book, you should use the Ordnance Survey Outdoor Leisure and Pathfinder maps and a reliable compass at all times when walking in the Lake District, even on these short walks. Be sure that you are able to use this combination correctly. Get into the habit of knowing where you are all the time, for some mutiple path intersections on lower ground, especially in forested areas in enclosed landscapes, can be confusing, while on the higher, open fellsides mist and cloud can blow in very quickly indeed, seriously restricting distant vision. All compass bearings have been taken to the nearest 22½ degree point, e.g. (N), (NNE), (NE), etc. This is considered to be sufficiently accurate over the relatively small distances travelled between the taking of successive readings. Take confirmatory compass bearings as necessary, particularly when the visibility is poor and/or you may become unsure of your exact position.

Ordnance Survey maps are excellent but not infallible. On rare occasions where there are differences between the route descriptions and the OS maps, rely on the route descriptions.

In addition, the human-constructed features of Lakeland are constantly changing: fences appear and disappear, K-gates replace L-stiles and vice versa, additional waymarker signs appear and others are removed. Should you come across isolated differences along the route from those described, presume that these have occurred since the book went to press, and proceed with confidence to the next certain feature described.

The heights of the major fells have been given in both metric and imperial measurements. The metric heights have been taken from the relevant, up-to-date Ordnance Survey maps. The imperial equivalents have been calculated by using a conversion factor of 0.3048m = 1 ft and have been rounded off to the nearest 5 ft.

Where there is more than one version of place names the spelling that appears on the Ordnance Survey Outdoor Leisure and Pathfinder maps has been used, unless otherwise indicated.

KESWICK, BORROWDALE AND THE NORTHERN FELLS

1 WHINLATTER FOREST PARK, BARF AND LORD'S SEAT

STARTING/ FINISHING POINT
Forest Visitor Centre, Whinlatter Pass OLM 4: MR 208245

GRADING OF WALK
Moderate/ challenging

TIME ALLOWANCE
4 hours

DISTANCE
7.3 km
(4½ miles)

TOTAL HEIGHT GAINED
250m (820ft)

HIGHEST POINT
Lord's Seat 552m
(1810ft)

Previous page: Bassenthwaite Lake observed from Barf.

GRADIENTS
There are two demanding uphill slopes: the final steep, craggy approach to the summit of Barf and the longer climb up more rounded fells to the top of Lord's Seat, which can become slippery in places

PARKING
Extensive and well-screened parking facilities

PUBLIC TRANSPORT
CMS bus routes 77 Keswick to Buttermere and 79 Seatoller, Keswick to Whinlatter (The Borrowdale Bus)

GENERAL
A forest guide map is available but a compass is essential for this walk. Most of the paths are good, but there are occasional boggy areas

TACKLING THE WALK

CASUAL WALKERS
This walk will provide a taste of the more exposed, higher fells. It also calls for navigational and route-finding skills through enclosed forestry plantations, where there are many choices of way, and across more open country, where landmarks which will confirm your position and correct continuation route will need to be identified. It is a walk which could well stimulate your appetite for more adventurous explorations of the fells, be these longer routes or walks over higher ground – or both.

FAMILY WALKERS
The full route is probably too long, too strenuous and too exposed for those with young children. However, it should appeal strongly to older youngsters, especially those in their early teens, as it will provide the necessary sense of adventure and challenge. Keep the very young to the safety of the clearly marked forest trails (of which there are plenty), including that part of the route which leads to the edge of the conifers at Beckstones Gill. In warm weather they can

14

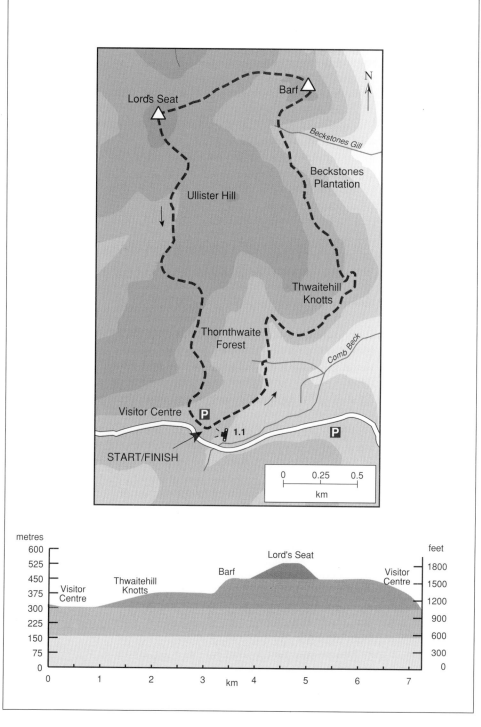

15

splash around here happily for some time, before you retrace your outward steps back to the many attractions of the Visitor Centre.

DEDICATED FELL WALKERS

The walk by way of Barf to Lord's Seat is interesting and provides some superb perspectives of the surrounding higher fells. There are plenty of opportunities for extending this route, including walking down to Thornthwaite beside Comb Beck and then climbing back up from the vicinity of Powter How alongside Beckstones Gill, thus passing by The Clerk and The Bishop's rocks *en route*. Another variant from the summit of Lord's Seat is to track around to the NW across Todd Fell and Broom Fell keeping to the higher ground, before circling back around Lorton Fells, crossing the B5292 road through Whinlatter Pass and then walking E above Whinlatter Gill back to the Visitor Centre.

FROM the picnic area at the far end of the Visitor Centre, walk E along the lower path of the second of two forks in the path. This leads away from the buildings and carpark, and passes junction marker post (JMP) 15 above on your L. You also pass a white-painted cottage almost immediately on your R as you make your way along a broad, gravel-surfaced forest trail which leads pleasantly downhill beneath mature coniferous trees – mostly Douglas fir. The obvious continuation way is then signed with trail marker posts, in which red- and blue-painted bands have been cut. To start with, the surrounding forest plantation obscures more distant landscapes, but further on convenient gaps in the foliage on your R allow some splendid early sightings of the fellsides sweeping towards Grisedale Pike, far above to the SW.

Keep to the broad track as it veers NE, ignoring a path leading off to your R before skirting a vehicle barrier. Bear L at the junction identified by JMP14 in order to maintain your height: alternatives mean regaining the lost height further on. The wide track twists and turns as it makes it way through the dense conifers. Watch out for descending cyclists along this section – they have a right to be there, but sensible speed limits are not always observed! The route then bends sharply R to cross a narrow valley which falls away to your R. Waymarked paths peel off here, blue bands downhill to the R and red bands uphill to the L. Pass by these as your broader, more level way straightens out to lead SE for a short distance, before bending back L towards the E again.

When you reach JMP11, veer L to continue walking slightly uphill, diverging from the narrower trail leading downhill on your R. The path continues along a fairly straight, diagonal stretch before reaching another acute bend, this one to the L. Carry on past this and, having climbed up on to higher ground, branch R at JMP9 and continue uphill, walking N before veering NW. The rising track eventually reaches more open terrain and along the next series of bends are the first clear sightings of the steep-sided, craggy slopes of Barf, rearing up ahead to the N. This is your next main objective. Sections of Bassenthwaite Lake also appear down below to the NE, while beyond the westerly slopes of Skiddaw tower up to the ENE. The satellite peaks of Ullock Pike, Longside Edge, Carl Side and Little Man are also revealed in clear weather. Further on, turn around to observe Keswick and The Dodds leading upwards to the summit of Helvellyn, far away to the ESE.

When you reach the fork at JMP8, bear R along the lower track, which leads more directly towards Barf. The route then winds around the fellside along a pleasant grassy way, dropping down progressively to reach the northern perimeter of the extensive Beckstones Plantation at Beckstones Gill (MR 213265). Avoiding a seductive grassy way off to your L, emerge from the trees by means of a stile over the wire boundary fence before crossing the stream directly below.

A narrow, rougher stony path leads further uphill from the indentation of the beck, traversing eastwards around the steep, bilberry- and heather-clad fellsides which rise towards the summit of Barf. As you gain more height, glance to your R to spot the northern part of Derwent Water to the SE with Bleaberry Fell rising beyond. The narrow but clearly defined path twists around grassy banks and over craggy outcrops to reach the summit of Barf. Keep a particularly tight rein on younger children along here and also on the summit itself, because there are potentially dangerous fallaways to the R of your approach.

In good weather the distant views from the top of this impressive, isolated crag are superb. Some you will have glimpsed earlier in the walk, but new vistas include a more complete exposure of Bassenthwaite Lake snaking away below to the N. Turning anticlockwise, in clear weather the summit of Lord's Seat – your next objective – rises impressively to the W above the vast, forested slopes which intervene. Also visible is the tip of Grisedale Pike rising serenely in the SW – quite magnificent.

Begin your descent from Barf along the obvious continuation footpath leading off NW. The way winds around a series of grassy hillocks before bearing L to cross a shallow depression more directly in line with Lord's Seat. The condition of the path varies along here, as sections of firm ground of compacted earth and stones become interlaced with patches of boggy, waterlogged terrain. The latter do demand some care in selecting the best way across or around as you approach them. From the hollow, the path snakes upwards again across more ranging fellsides, tracking SW and then

*1.1 Whinlatter
Forest Visitor
Centre.*

wsw over peaty slopes, which in places can become slippery after prolonged rain. These inclines lead to the summit of Lord's Seat, at 552m (1810ft) the highest point of the route. The final climb to the top is quite demanding, as the gradient steepens and rougher, often waterlogged ground has to be crossed, so take your time, pace yourself and arrive at the summit in good shape to admire the new panoramas visible from here. In good weather the expansive mountain scenery includes Grisedale Pike (s), Hopegill Head (ssw), Lorton Vale (wsw), Greystones (w), Broom Fell (nw) and Barf, Skiddaw and Little Man (ene).

When you have seen enough, turn l from your approach direction and head down southwards across the grassy fellsides, keeping to a narrow but clearly defined track. This line of descent will quickly lead you to a wooden stile across a wire fence. Over this, the continuation path has been renovated in parts by the insertion of wooden latticeworks over what were previously most exacting sections of the way. The descent continues towards some attractive clumps of spruce, which you penetrate a short distance further on as the way bends l and towards the e where more sections of latticework ease the going underfoot. You then pass JMP6 on your l, and at the following JMP5 be careful to branch r along the narrow path which leads southwards in the direction of Grisedale Pike.

The way snakes further downhill across open, heather-smothered slopes, skirting above another extensive forested plantation sweeping down to your r. The exact boundary of the densely packed conifers changes as harvesting operations in the forest are undertaken. There is an excellent gravel path along here which is firm, dry and secure. Further on, this is swapped for an equally pleasant grassy track, followed by reversion to a stony path. These tracks make their way around the fellside, bearing l to pass an area of sapling spruce before the route bends back to the r to be joined by another track coming in from an acute angle on the L. The path continues to lose height, twisting around toward the sw.

Turn l and towards the se when you reach one of the main roads through the forest ahead, and follow the path as it continues to lose height. You will pass JMP3, which is also identified as Tarbarrel Moss. The way then leads southwards down through Thornthwaite Forest in the direction of Grisedale Pike. Keep to the wide track as it descends back towards the Visitor Centre below, ignoring a succession of paths off to both l and r, until you reach the next major junction of forest roadways. A seat has been thoughtfully positioned here, together with JMP2. In clear weather there are more revealing views from here towards Grisedale Pike, but in low cloud consult the helpful picture board, which graphically reveals the obscured panorama.

From this spot, select the path leading down southwards. This starts from the R of the picture board as you look towards Grisedale Pike. Return to the grounds of the Visitor Centre by turning L and following the branch path that leads through a recently constructed adventure playground adorned with artificial moles and toadstools.

PLACES AND ACTIVITIES OF INTEREST

WHINLATTER FOREST PARK AND VISITOR CENTRE

Whinlatter Forest Park, one of the Forestry Commission's oldest forests, is purported to be England's only Mountain Forest. The Visitor Centre is the ideal place from which to start your exploration as here films, hands-on computers, a unique working model and other exhibits depict the life of a working forest. There is an education and information service, and staff will help you plan your day in the forest. There is also a gift shop and tearoom, and classroom facilities are provided for visiting groups. Walkers, orienteers and cyclists are well catered for, and children can create their own fun in the forest playground or try one of the junior trails such as the Rabbit Run or Fox Trot. Maps, control cards and achievement certificates are available.

The Visitor Centre is open daily. For further information contact Whinlatter Visitor Centre (see Useful Addresses)

THE BISHOP'S ROCK

In 1783 the newly appointed Bishop of Derry, now Londonderry, was travelling to Whitehaven to take passage to his diocese in Ireland. Breaking his journey at The Swan, over a few drinks he bet his fellow guests he could ride his pack pony to the top of Barf and on to Lord's Seat.

He reached the rock, now known as The Bishop's Rock, where the pony stumbled and fell, killing itself and the rider. They were buried at the foot of the scree. The rock marking this spot is known as The Clerk. The landlord of the inn had the rocks whitewashed, and this tradition is continued to the present day. The payment to the person(s) who whitewashed the stones was 5 shillings and a quart of ale, but today this price is negotiable annually!

These two rocks may also be observed/visited by walking just a short distance from Powter How carpark (MR 221266), and this may be combined easily with a visit to Whinlatter.

2 CASTLERIGG STONE CIRCLE AND ST JOHN'S IN THE VALE CHURCH

STARTING/ FINISHING POINT
Castlerigg Stone Circle, about 2.5km (1½ miles) E of the centre of Keswick
OLM 4: MR 291236

GRADING OF WALK
Moderate/ challenging

TIME ALLOWANCE
3 hours

DISTANCE
6.4 km (4 miles)

TOTAL HEIGHT GAINED
180m (590ft)

HIGHEST ELEVATION POINT
Low Rigg
260m (855ft)

GRADIENTS
The gradients are fairly gentle and gradual, and are well spaced out

PARKING
Vehicle layby opposite the entrance to Castlerigg Stone Circle holds 15–20 cars

PUBLIC TRANSPORT
Not on a bus route, but there are excellent transport links to nearby Keswick (see Walk 3)

GENERAL
Most of the paths are clear and well drained, although some sections may become muddy after prolonged rain. The route includes numerous gates and stiles, and route finding needs care in places

TACKLING THE WALK

CASUAL WALKERS

This is an ideal exploration for the majority of walkers. The route is continuously full of interest, and with modest gradients it should appeal to those who like to wander across the open spaces of the lower fells, having these to themselves for much of the way. The walk is also suitable for testing and improving navigational skills in countryside where, if you make the odd mistake, this can quickly be rectified without encountering potential hazards.

FAMILY WALKERS

In good weather, when the ground is firm underfoot, this is a walk which can be enjoyed by the entire family. It starts with some interesting boulders and passes by a delightful tarn, both of which should appeal strongly to children. The adults will find additional interest in the visit to St John's in the Vale Church.

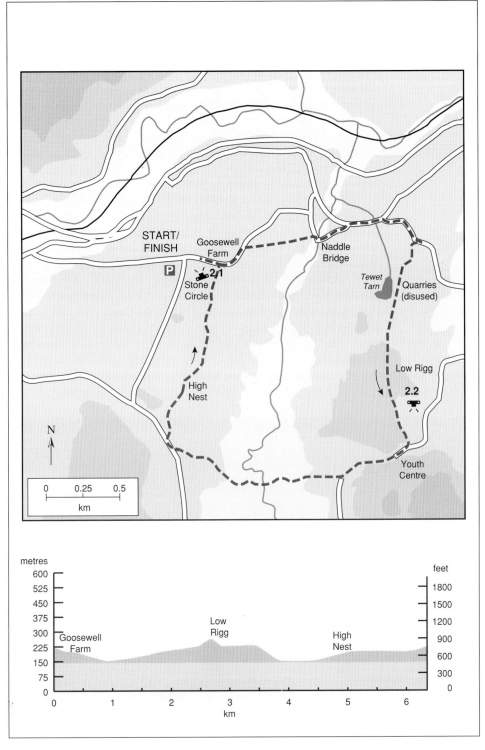

DEDICATED FELL WALKERS

Although relatively short and undemanding, this walk should appeal to many serious walkers due to its numerous and varied points of interest and superb views of the surrounding, higher fells. It could make a pleasant, relaxing evening stroll for this group of walkers. Alternatively, the walk could be extended southwards along the craggy spur of High Rigg, before looping back to the church by means of the footpaths through St John's in the Vale, using those nearest to the E flank of the ridge.

THE impressive Castlerigg Stone Circle is located in a flat, elevated field above Keswick and although this is not particularly high above the sprawling town it commands unrestricted panoramas in all directions. In clear weather the views are breathtaking, with high, craggy fells surrounding the circle of stones like some far-off amphitheatre. Start by looking towards Skiddaw to the NNW and slowly turn around clockwise to identify the following well-known peaks: Blencathra (NE), Great Dodd (SE), Helvellyn (SSE), High Rigg (SSE), Cat Bells and Red Pike (SW), Causey Pike (WSW), and Grisedale Pike (W). When you have seen enough, return to the adjacent lane where you parked your vehicle and turn R, heading E towards The Dodds.

2.1 Castlerigg Stone Circle and the slopes leading to Skiddaw.

The tree-fringed minor lane drops downhill, and when this curves to the L ignore the footpath off on your R signed to The Nest

(this is part of your return way). Keep walking along the lane until you reach Goosewell Farm with its assortment of light industrial units, including Packhorse Steelcraft. Branch off R here along the public footpath. This is accessed through a metal gate. (During the summer months you may find a sign attached to this gate requesting that you follow an alternative route which avoids growing crops. As a goodwill gesture to the farmer, continue down the road for about a further 200 paces, turn R over the stile and walk along the permitted, descending path, keeping near to the wall to connect with the normal route to the L of a gate and piped gutter). Walk down the field, selecting a diagonal to your L to pass through a second gate to the R of an electricity-cable support post. Maintain your direction by walking due E across the next large meadow and then head for the road bridge now in view below. This part of the route is through open landscapes of gentle, sheltered pastures sprinkled with attractive clumps of deciduous trees.

Next, pass through the gate in the stone wall on your L and then immediately cross the small watercourse by means of a bridge of aged wooden beams. Maintain your direction and cross the next stone wall by an S-stile, cut across the corner of the adjacent field and use the awkwardly positioned W-stile ahead to return to the surfaced lane. Turn R along this to cross Naddle Bridge (MR 300238) and continue along the winding roadway as it climbs uphill. Turn R when you reach the road junction ahead, using a grassy path to cut the corner. Keep to the grassy edge as you walk uphill and turn R at the next road turning. This is comprehensively signed to Shundraw - St John's in the Vale Church - Diocesan Youth Centre.

The lane bends sharply R before curving back L; after this, turn off along the public footpath on your R signed to St John's in the Vale Church via Tewit Tarn, which is accessed through a gate. From here, follow the grassy cart track as it winds uphill. The way then passes through a gap in a dry stone wall and continues along the clear track further up the bank beside another stone wall to your R. Pass by a directional post and walk down towards the tarn, which now comes into view ahead. Walk around the E shore, with the tarn on your R. In fine weather there are plenty of distant views from here, and the tranquil waters of the tarn make a particularly photogenic foreground.

Continue southwards from the tarn, heading up the gentle grassy slope. The narrowing track then leads to a stile over a wire fence, positioned to the R of a gate. During this approach the summit of Bleaberry Fell, overlooking Derwent Water to the W, looms up straight ahead on the far horizon. In negotiating this stile, watch out for the concealed strand of barbed wire pinned to the far side of the top board! Continue SSW further up the grassy track, towards

25

far-away Bleaberry Fell. Keep along the fainter trail as it bears L and due S and then, towards the top of the saddle, veer L to pass over the grassy ridge of Low Rigg. At 260m (855ft) this is the highest point of the route. Over this brow you can pick out the higher ground of High Rigg further S, and nestling below this craggy ridge is St John's in the Vale Church, your next main objective. The church is surrounded by a mixed group of sheltering trees in an otherwise fairly barren landscape.

Cross the stone wall ahead by means of the S-stile at the point indicated by yellow arrowheads, and walk the remaining short distance down to the church along the obvious way, which leads SSE. Be careful, however, to avoid all side paths off to both L and R. Finally, use the W-stile to reach the lane leading past the church. St John's in the Vale Church has a colourful history recorded in a helpful information leaflet, and its simple and serene interior deserves thorough scrutiny. The friendly invitation to do just this

reads: 'This church is always open, please go in – To say a prayer – To sit quietly – To look around.' Afterwards, continue sw along the lane, passing by the associated Youth Centre of the Carlisle Diocesan. You will then reach a K-gate, before the track descends quite steeply in a series of twists and turns towards Sykes Farm, below to your R. Pass through another K-gate at the bottom of the brow, this one being positioned at the entrance to the farm, and cross the meadowland ahead to reach the main A591 road at Nest Brow (MR 290225) just over 1km (⅝ mile) further on. The first part of this relatively complicated section continues downhill, where the grassy trail threads through some more sheltered lowland countryside.

After yet another K-gate, the route continues across fields of growing crops where you are requested to keep strictly to the paths. The correct way is particularly well directed along here, to the extent that a signpost is positioned in the middle of a field to

2.2 Approaching St John's in the Vale Church.

indicate a right-angled turn NW towards Keswick at this point. When you reach the far edge of the field, a yellow arrowhead indicates that you should keep to the wire fence on your R to avoid passing through a farm gateway. Beyond a gap ahead, a small stream is crossed by means of a gated, wooden footbridge positioned in the shade of a young sycamore tree.

Cross the next field, keeping to a due W diagonal and making for a signpost directly ahead. This is positioned close to a second watercourse, which you also cross. From here, continue along the wide, distinct track before passing through the first gateway on your L. Head up the next field, keeping close to the fence, and then the stone wall, on your immediate R. Use the flight of steps to cross the final wall at the top of the field, before walking the remaining short distance to reach the main A591 road. This links Keswick and Ambleside, and is accessed through a G-stile in a stone wall.

Turn R to continue along the grass verge beside the busy road. However, after about 50 paces turn off R along the signed public footpath, in the form of a track, which leads down to Low Nest Farm. Immediately after crossing a cattle grid, turn L to climb over a stile and continue along the signed footpath. Walk uphill on a diagonal to your R which leads NNE. Head towards the trees above to cross another stile, this one positioned beneath trees and spanning a wire fence. Turn R beyond this stile and walk down the lane towards the buildings of High Nest. Pass between them and exit through the gate just beyond the stone barn.

The continuation way is now NE, initially beside a stone wall on your R, which further on gives way to a hawthorn hedge. Skirt around a small plantation of fir trees and then cross another stone wall by means of an L-stile. Two more of these follow, each bridging stone walls running at right angles to your approach. The way is now dead in line with the slopes and arêtes of Blencathra (Saddleback), rising majestically in the far distance. It leads NNE towards another copse of trees, and the ground rises marginally as you bear L of the plantation to follow a narrow path of compacted earth. This connects at a gate with the lane you used at the start of your outward journey. Turn L and walk the short distance back to the vehicle layby.

PLACES AND ACTIVITIES OF INTEREST

CASTLERIGG STONE CIRCLE

Dating from late Neolithic or Bronze age, this site is owned by the National Trust, who also manage the property under a guardianship arrangement with English Heritage. Including the Sanctuary, the circle is comprised of 50 'stones' – actually large boulders. It is constructed of local stone and glacial deposits from distant outcrops deposited in the area during the last Ice Age. A place of mystery and solitude, the circle is believed to have been built for several separate purposes. These include religious enactments, as a designated meeting place for gatherings of nearby Neolithic tribes and as an important observation platform for surveying seasonal movements of the sun and moon. In a detailed examination of British stone circles, Professor A. Thom identified two 'sighting' lines at Castlerigg: one marks sunrise over High Rigg on the date now known as Candlemas (2 February) and the other sunset over Skiddaw at the Winter Solstice (22 December).

TEWET (ALSO TEWIT OR TEWFIT) TARN

Tewet Tarn (MR 304236) is located at 205m (675ft) above sea level and has a maximum depth of about 2m (6ft). It is roughly oval in shape and, although not particularly large, is situated in a commanding setting, occupying a shelf in the undulating, grassy fellside. In fine weather, when the water is still, the surface captures reflections of the surrounding high fells which are quite superb, particularly when these summits are mantled in snow. The tarn and its shores support spike rush, water lobelia, pondweed, water horsetail and sedge, the latter providing a haven for coot; the tarn is also often visited by peewits.

ST JOHN'S IN THE VALE CHURCH

It is not certain how long there has been a church on this site, but it was one of the five Chapels of Crosthwaite. The present construction dates from 1845 but incorporates sections of much older buildings; according to some scholars, there is a possibility that it dates back to the thirteenth century. This conjecture is through a reference in the Chartulary of Fountain's Abbey to *domus sancti Johannis* – a house of St John. From the outside, the church, tucked away among the surrounding fells, is simple and unassuming and many may wonder why it is located at such an apparently inaccessible and impractical spot. However, the minor road which now passes the church was once an important communications link between Matterdale and Wanthwaite, when the church served the two communities on either side of the intervening fell. The inside of the church is described as 'warm and homely with an atmosphere conducive to peace and prayer'. There are many unique features, including the Royal Arms of George III, panelling to pew height, pulpit and sounding board, sanctuary rails and chair, altar, vicar's desk, font, bell tower and several other memorials of interest.

3 BOAT TRIPS ON DERWENT WATER AND LAKESIDE WALK TO LODORE FALLS

STARTING/ FINISHING POINT
Landing stages towards the N tip of Derwent Water at Keswick. OLM 4: MR 264227. The walk starts from Hawes End landing stage at Kitchen Bay (MR 251213) and finishes at Lodore landing stage (MR 265192)

GRADING OF WALK
Easy/ straightforward

TIME ALLOWANCE
2 hours

DISTANCE
4.6km (2.9 miles)

TOTAL HEIGHT GAINED
20m (65ft)

HIGHEST POINT
Lodore Falls
60m (195ft)

GRADIENTS
Virtually flat, apart from the climb to observe Lodore Falls

PARKING
Extensive parking facilities are conveniently positioned near the lakeside

PUBLIC TRANSPORT
Keswick is well served by CMS bus routes from all directions, including services 77 Buttermere to Keswick, 79 Whinlatter to Seatoller, 108 Patterdale via Penrith linking with X5 to Keswick, 555 Lancaster to Carlisle, and X5 Penrith to Whitehaven

GENERAL
The paths are good and elevated duckboards span most wet or boggy patches. The land surrounding the southern end of Derwent Water may become flooded and impassable after prolonged heavy rain

TACKLING THE WALK

CASUAL WALKERS
This is an easy, undemanding walk with plenty of interest and fantastic views. It is therefore an ideal walk for the vast majority of casual walkers, particularly those who enjoy strolling through woodland, spotting birds and mammals, and relaxing beside sheltered waters.

FAMILY WALKERS
With two boat trips, every opportunity to stop and mess about by the water's edge, and the added attraction of seeing an impressive waterfall and perhaps being allowed to take a canoe or other craft out on Derwent Water, this walk is a must for those with children. Given fine weather – and it is worth selecting a day when this is likely if you possibly can – this is a walk where it is almost guaranteed that the whole family will thoroughly enjoy themselves.

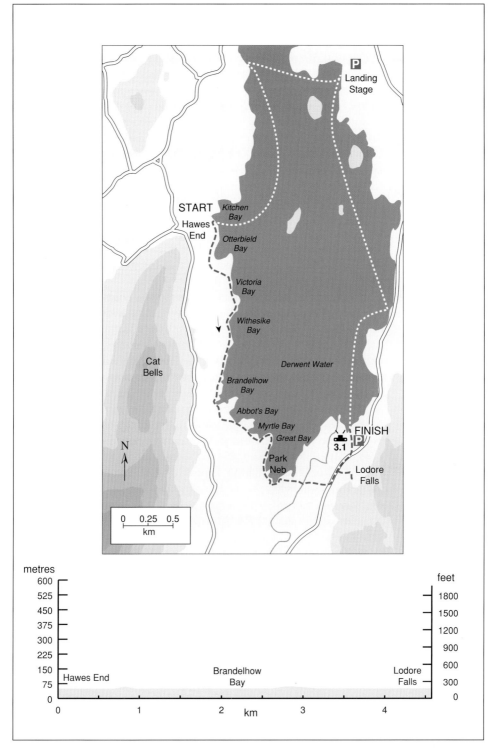

START
Hawes
End

Kitchen
Bay

Otterbield
Bay

Victoria
Bay

Withesike
Bay

Cat
Bells

Brandelhow
Bay

Abbot's Bay

Myrtle Bay

Great Bay

Park
Neb

Derwent Water

Landing
Stage

FINISH
3.1

Lodore
Falls

N

0   0.25   0.5
km

metres
600
525
450
375
300
225
150
75
0

Hawes End

Brandelhow
Bay

Lodore
Falls

0   1   2   km   3   4

feet
1800
1500
1200
900
600
300
0

DEDICATED FELL WALKERS

This is one to squeeze in between strenuous days spent among the high fells, when you feel like a break from continuously scaling demanding slopes and are content to settle for a relaxing time on the flat. However, if this is not for you, the walk may be extended in a number of ways. For example, you could climb right to the top of the Lodore Falls and then continue up the valley as far as Watendlath, or you could walk back into Keswick – perhaps even both! Another possibility from the Hawes End jetty is to scale Cat Bells and then continue s along the rising ridge over Maiden Moor, High Spy and on to Dale Head.

THE outing starts with a boat trip across Derwent Water from the landing stages at Keswick. Select one of the launches operated by Keswick Launch which sail – at frequent intervals in summer – anti-clockwise around the lake.

Derwent Water is regarded by many as the jewel in the crown of the English Lakes and the trip across its clear waters is very pleasant. In fine weather there is ample opportunity while afloat to locate many of the high fells surrounding Derwent Water, as well as other landmarks which border the lake. Immediately after your departure from Keswick and to your rear, the massive, rounded fell-sides rising to the summit of Skiddaw dominate the skyline to the N. Ahead and to the R are the long, finger-like green spurs of the North Westerly Fells raking down towards the lake. These ridges contain the prominent and well-known pointed peaks of Cat Bells (SW), Causey Pike (WSW) and Grisedale Pike (W). Barf and The Bishop's Rock (see Walk 1) appear over to the R, to the NW. The view southwards up the lake is through the jaws of Borrowdale and beyond towards the highest fells of the central massif, rising impressively to Scafell Pike – at 978m (3210ft) the highest elevation in England.

Having glided silently past tree-covered Derwent Isle, disembark from the launch at Hawes End, Kitchen Bay. From the landing stage, head across the shingle bay on your L, walking southwards around Derwent Water. Then connect with the lakeside path, just above to your R. Keep to this path as it hugs the shoreline, meandering around the bays and indents, across the headlands and promontories, tracking southwards along the w shores of the lake. Presently, to your rear, the knife-like arêtes of Blencathra (Saddleback) come into view, punctuating the skies across the water to the NE. Otterbield Bay is soon reached, and is exited via a P-stile positioned beneath a beech tree. After this, ignore the grassy side path leading off on the R.

From here, excellent well-drained paths extend further s through both wooded areas and clearings. These lead to another P-stile, this one next to a wooden gate. After this, follow the way around to the R, avoiding an alternative off to the L. The correct route leads back down to the lakeside and to the jetty located at Low Brandelhow. Turn R here, pass through the K-gate and continues along the lakeside path. A succession of delightful bays and wooded headlands follow; keep to the main path nearest to the lake, ignoring all paths leading off on your R. The surrounding woodlands contain an attractive mixture of oak, beech, holly, larch and Scots pine and scaling the occasional rocky outcrop will add to the overall interest of the walk.

You next pass the landing stage at High Brandelhow, a National Trust property, and from here the Lodore Swiss Hotel with its famous falls, secreted away out of sight in the steep, wooded fell-sides above, may be located across the lake to the SE. The obvious way tracks around the craggy, narrow promontory of Brandelhow Point to reach Abbot's Bay. This involves crossing a small indent, after which the path leads to a swing gate. Through this, bear L to continue again along the path nearest to the water's edge. There are alternative ways along here, but make sure your chosen route also leads s close to the lakeside. These alternative paths merge further on, to pass between a wooden shed and a secluded cottage named Brandelhow. Veer L after this to pass through a K-gate.

3.1 Lodore landing stage, Derwent Water.

Next, bypass the private drive leading to the superbly situated residence named Abbot's Bay House by bearing R along a wide gravel way. You then walk through the somewhat enclosed landscape of Manesty Park, before reaching a stone building located on the fringe of the woodland. Turn L opposite this building, following the path signed to Lodore. You will then encounter the first of several sections of elevated duckboards across muddy patches. Just beyond this, be vigilant to spot and follow the faint, narrow path leading off beneath trees on your L. This ascends craggy ground along an attractively wooded promontory to bring you to a vantage point at the tip of the narrow headland, where an unusual slate form has been positioned. With its unrestricted views across Derwent Water, this sheltered area presents the perfect picnic place.

Your journey continues southwards around the lake, now along a grassy path which leads through more mixed woodlands and back to the main interconnection of pathways. Turn L along these, always choosing paths nearest to the water's edge in order to retain the best unrestricted views across the lake. Cross a P-stile and continue around Great Bay at the southern tip of the lake, passing by a promontory named Park Neb. In this section, avoid a path off to the R. The route then crosses the wide, open, glaciated valley of Borrowdale, through which the River Derwent meanders before spilling its contents into Derwent Water. The river is crossed at a particularly attractive, narrow arched bridge. Look ahead when approaching and leaving this bridge to spot the skilful manoeuvres of intrepid climbers scaling the near-vertical rock pitches of Shepherds Crag, high above.

An obvious way now leads across low-lying pastures to the B5289 road through Borrowdale; this connection is made at MR 263187. Turn L along the footpath at the near side of the road, walking northwards in the direction of Keswick to reach toilet facilities. Then cross over the road and turn off R to pass by Lodore House, just before reaching the main Lodore Swiss Hotel building. Walk around and behind the hotel, following signs 'To the Falls' to pass by an honesty box where you are encouraged to leave 5p per person! Cross over the stream, Watendlath Beck, and then follow the rough, stony path which leads steeply uphill by the side of the rocky, tree-covered ravine through which the waters tumble. The path will bring you to the bottom of the falls amid boulder-strewn ground.

There is a series of separate cascades and you can continue by the side of these along a secure path for as far and as high as you like. When you have had enough, simply turn around and retrace your outward steps back to the road. On approaching it, take particular care of young children as the entrance comes suddenly and at a blind spot. Turn R along the road, either to enter the hotel for refreshments or to continue past it to reach, immediately after this, the entrance lane on your L which leads down to Lodore landing stage. This is your embarkation point for the return boat trip back to Keswick. At this landing stage there is an approved centre which provides canoeing, dragon boating, kayaking, sailing and windsurfing instruction and hire.

The return trip on one of the Keswick Launch boats will take you past impressive rock faces, sheltered, secluded bays and wooded islands back to your starting point, the jetties at Keswick.

PLACES AND ACTIVITIES OF INTEREST

KESWICK LAUNCH ON DERWENT WATER

Weather permitting, Keswick Launch operate clockwise and anti-clockwise sailings round Derwent Water between seven convenient stopping locations. From March to November, motor launches depart at approximately hourly intervals from 10am onwards, with a restricted service operating from December to February. Special family saver fares (up to two adults and three children) are available and evening cruises take place from May to September.

For further details or to obtain a timetable, contact Derwent Water Launch Co Ltd, Keswick (see Useful Addresses).

LODORE SWISS HOTEL AND FALLS

Parts of the famous Lodore Swiss Hotel (now owned by the Stakis group) date back to the seventeenth century, when it was known as the Lodore Inn. The inn, hotel and falls have featured in many guides to the English Lakes, starting with Budsworth's *A Fortnight's Ramble to the Lakes,* published in 1795, which contains the mention, 'We landed near a public house and walked up to a ruinous mill at the foot of Lodore Waterfall'. Tom Gleeson, the knowledgeable present-day hall porter, has compiled an interesting short history of the hotel and falls, and he is quite generous in handing out copies of this to guests and to those using the hotel facilities. The falls are privately owned and an honesty box is provided for contributions towards the upkeep of the paths etc.

For further details, contact the Stakis Keswick Lodore (see Useful Addresses, contact telephone numbers).

PLATTY: CANOES AND KAYAKS

Operating from the boat landings at Lodore, Platty – an organization approved by the British Canoe Union (BCU) – offers tuition and hire of Canadian canoes, single and double kayaks, Laser 16, Topper, Oppy or Pico sailing boats, windsurfers and a dragon boat holding 20 people, for use on Derwent Water. Buoyancy aids are included in the tuition and hire rates.

For more information and rates of charge, contact Platty (see Useful Addresses, contact telephone numbers).

THE WESTERN DALES AND FELLS

4 AROUND BUTTERMERE

**STARTING/
FINISHING POINT**
Lower carpark
Buttermere village,
OLM 4: MR 173169

**GRADING OF
WALK**
Easy/
straightforward

TIME ALLOWANCE
2½ hours

DISTANCE
7km (4.4 miles)

**TOTAL HEIGHT
GAINED**
45m (150ft)

HIGHEST POINT
Around the lake
120m (395ft)

GRADIENTS
None of any consequence

PARKING
The lower carpark holds up to 40 cars, with coach-parking facilities in the village. There are additional parking areas above the village and toilets close by

PUBLIC TRANSPORT
CMS bus route 77 Keswick to Buttermere village

GENERAL
The paths are all good to excellent, with virtually no waterlogging

TACKLING THE WALK

CASUAL WALKERS

This undemanding, low-level walk around Buttermere amid spectacular mountain scenery should satisfy the expectations of the most discerning walker. The route is full of interest, the views are terrific, and the extensive wildlife will appeal particularly to those keen on bird spotting.

FAMILY WALKERS

The trip to Buttermere and a leisurely stroll around this gem of a lake is considered a must for all families who are keen on walking or who revel in the great outdoors. In fine, sunny weather, you could spend most of the day here, taking binoculars, a fishing net and towels with you.

DEDICATED FELL WALKERS

The walk around Buttermere can be combined with longer routes in a number of ways. It forms part of the circular walk from the village up on to Hay Stacks and back via Scarth Gap, plus most variants of this route. Alternatively, it can be completed as a half-day

Previous pages:
*Autumn tints at
Buttermere.*

38

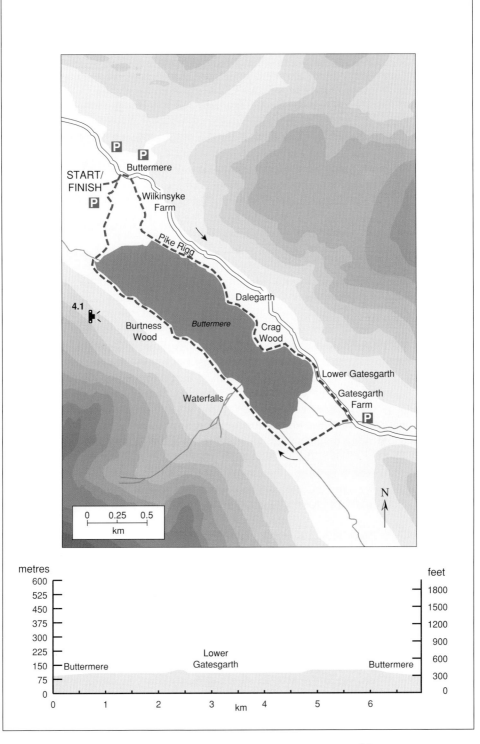

START/
FINISH

Buttermere

Wilkinsyke
Farm

Pike Rigg

Dalegarth

4.1

Burtness
Wood

Buttermere

Crag
Wood

Lower Gatesgarth

Gatesgarth
Farm

Waterfalls

N

| 0 | 0.25 | 0.5 |
km

metres

600
525
450
375
300
225
150 — Buttermere
75
0

Lower
Gatesgarth

Buttermere

feet

1800
1500
1200
900
600
300
0

0   1   2   3   km   4   5   6

walk combined with a contrasting quick climb to the summit of Grasmoor by way of Whiteless Pike. For those staying in Buttermere, the walk itself presents a delightful evening stroll after a hard day spent among the higher fells.

FROM the carpark, walk back through the centre of the tiny hamlet, passing by the Fish Inn and the Bridge Hotel to reach the B5289. Turn R along this road, walking uphill and with St James' Church in view further up the slope, then turn R along the farm lane signed 'Public bridleway – Lakeshore path'. Follow this to pass through Syke Farm, named Wilkinsyke Farm on the OLM. The path leads you between a cottage and the quaint farm buildings to an exit gate at the far end of the farm, where the continuation way is reassuringly signed 'Footpath'. Pause here to look above to your R to locate High Crag, High Stile and the 'Saddle' of Red Pike, all towering above towards the s. The lower slopes of this mighty ridge are liberally covered with acres of coniferous forests and deciduous woodland, and you will walk through part of these on your way back.

The wide track threads beneath oak and ash trees and soon, above to your L, the expansive fellsides leading towards the summit of Robinson appear to the E. Almost directly ahead, in fine weather the multi-domed summit of Hay Stacks comes into view to the SSE, while behind you to the R the whaleback shape of Mellbreak dominates the distant vistas to the NW. To the L of this is the more pointed profile of Hen Comb, to the WNW. A short distance further on, look behind you to the N, where in favourable weather part of the ridge leading to Whiteless Pike, with the huge bulk of Grasmoor towering above, completes the arena of mountains surrounding and screening Buttermere.

You next pass a National Trust sign which, if you have the inclination to read it thoroughly, will make you an almost instant expert on Herdwick sheep! Turn full R when you reach the next gateway, to continue along the lakeshore path. From this point, the continuation way leads gently down towards Buttermere beside a wire fence. Through the gate ahead, a short, rocky stepway leads further down the slope to then swing L, more directly in line with the water. Pass through a K-gate and follow a permitted footpath of compacted earth that winds SE through shady, mixed woodland, with oak predominating.

A really delightful section of comfortable walking stretches ahead along a clear and secure path heading eastwards towards the SE end of the lake. In clear, sunny weather, particularly when there is a dusting of snow on the tops, the continuous views are supreme, and convenient gaps in the foliage provide glimpses

across the lake of Hay Stacks and the various peaks constituting the High Stile ridge. Several K-gates are negotiated before you reach a rounded, wooded promontory which juts out into the lake. There is a shingle beach at this spot which children may like to investigate, while a mixture of mature trees including lime, oak and sycamore will provide shade for the adults.

Normally, you now have to pass through a narrow, dark tunnel carved through a rocky headland. At the time of writing, Hassness tunnel is closed due to an unstable rockslide. It is hoped it will be reopened as soon as possible, but in the meantime a signed diversion way around this impasse must be followed. Pass this, ignore a side path leading uphill and negotiate two more K-gates, to reach another sweep of shaded shingle beach. Cross a small watercourse by a wooden footbridge, and then around the next bend the famous Buttermere Pines, purported to be the most photographed trees in the whole of Lakeland, come into view sheltering the southernmost tip of the lake. A gateway follows, together with a reminder notice that this shoreline path is available by permission of the landowner. Walking around the final bay of the lake before you are forced on to the road provides a grand climax to this section, particularly in May, when the brilliant yellows and ochres of nearby gorse in full bloom provide a perfect foreground for the more distant steep, rocky spur of Fleetwith Pike, which stands sentinel over the SE end of Buttermere.

4.1 Buttermere observed during the descent from Red Pike.

41

When you reach the brow ahead, bear R to keep along the permitted lakeshore path and, after passing through another K-gate and crossing a small stream via a wooden plank bridge, you will reach the B5289 at MR 191155. Bear R along this road to walk southwards towards the pines. Keep to the road for about 0.5km (¼ mile) until you arrive at Gatesgarth Farm, keeping to the footpath-of-sorts wherever possible in order to avoid oncoming traffic. Use the road bridge to cross Gatesgarthdale Beck and then turn immediately R to reconnect with the continuation of the lakeside path. There is quite an amusing notice positioned at the entrance gate to this path, which helpfully informs you that the nearest toilets are at Buttermere village – 3.2km (2 miles) away!

The route continues along a section of public bridleway, which skirts around the farm to the L. Pass through the gate bearing a sign 'Lakeside Path' to walk along a broad, pebbly way that leads across flat meadowland towards the High Stile fells directly ahead. This part of the route is particularly well signed and you are quite reasonably requested to keep to the designated way. Through more K-gates, the obvious route leads to the base of Scarth Gap Pass, which tracks over into upper Ennerdale. Turn R here to avoid the higher ground and to continue along the public bridleway back towards Buttermere village. However, your now gravel path does take you marginally uphill to the NW. Further on, the way is consolidated by another diagonal path coming in on your L, over from Scarth Gap.

From here, the route leads through wild, open landscapes with continuous fine views across Buttermere towards the steep fellsides culminating in Robinson and, further ahead on your R, the even larger bulk of Grasmoor, rising to the N. The path crosses Comb Beck, with its miniature waterfalls cascading down the craggy fellsides, and simultaneously skirts a small group of fir trees. There is a choice of continuation ways leading NW alongside the lake, and these include a higher bridleway and paths nearer to the water's edge. The latter are preferable for most walkers as they provide more open views across the lake.

If you have kept to the wider bridleway higher up, this leads to a gate positioned in the stone boundary wall of an extensive area of mixed woodland named Burtness Wood. Select the right-hand path at the fork ahead and follow this back down towards the lake. At the bottom of the slope, bear L to resume progress along the lakeside footpath, now walking NW under a dense canopy of tall fir trees. This delightful path continues to wind round the boulder-strewn lakeside. A short distance further on, the attractive buildings of Buttermere village come back into view again across the waters of the lake. To the N of your present position, the craggy spur running E to W is the narrow escarpment of Rannerdale Knotts, while the ridge leading up further to the R culminates in Whiteless Pike and from there on to either Grasmoor or Crag Hill.

Keep to the fairly level paths near to the lake and avoid tracks on your L up steeply rising ground, as these lead towards Red Pike high above. When you reach the NW tip of the lake, turn R to pass through a gate, then cross Buttermere Dubs by the wooden bridge and follow the obvious connecting footpaths across the low-lying meadows to arrive back in Buttermere village, now only some 0.5km (¼ mile) away. In your final approach to the village you will often pass a parked Land Rover manned by helpful National Trust personnel. This serves as a twin information and recruitment point, and if any queries have cropped up during your walk around the lake you should address your enquiries to these people.

PLACES AND ACTIVITIES OF INTEREST

BUTTERMERE VILLAGE

The small, attractive village of Buttermere nestles in a secluded valley, superbly positioned between two lakes among flat, lush green pastures. Buttermere lake lies to the SE and Crummock Water to the NW. An amphitheatre of high, craggy fells surrounds and encloses the village and these lakes, contributing to the remoteness of the splendid mountainous setting of this much-visited sheltered valley. The fascinating, tiny Parish Church of St James, just above the village, deserves your patronage, and two excellent hostelries, the Fish Inn and the Bridge Hotel, add to the general appeal of the place.

ST JAMES' CHURCH

Standing above Buttermere village, the tiny church of St James is built upon rock, a particularly solid foundation for any faith. It was built in 1884 to serve the Parish of Brigham, which then contained only 37 homes. The interior of the church is stunningly simple with narrow lancet windows, the altar one comprised of attractive stained glass depicting tiny statuettes of Mary and Martha. The present upgraded accoutrements are the tasteful work of the Rev. G. A. K. Hervey MA, carried out from 1929 to 1930.

5 AROUND ENNERDALE WATER

STARTING/ FINISHING POINT
Forestry
Commission carpark
to the W of
Ennerdale Water
OLM 4: MR 085154

GRADING OF WALK
Moderate/
challenging

TIME ALLOWANCE
4½ hours

DISTANCE
12.5 km
(7.8 miles)

TOTAL HEIGHT GAINED
30m (100ft)

HIGHEST POINT
Anglers' Crag
130m (425ft)

GRADIENTS
There is one modest ascent around Anglers' Crag

PARKING
Secluded parking beneath trees which holds 15-20 cars. An additional parking area nearer to the lake has recently been established

PUBLIC TRANSPORT
Not on a bus route

GENERAL
The paths are mostly firm and clear, with the occasional rough section but no boggy or waterlogged ground. The signs are adequate, where most needed

TACKLING THE WALK

CASUAL WALKERS

The route is suitable for most grades of walkers and, with the magnificent scenery and a chance really to flex your leg muscles and enjoy the thrill of some controlled exposure on rocks, it presents an ideal opportunity to test your taste for more adventurous explorations into the higher Lakeland fells.

FAMILY WALKERS

The full route is suitable for hardy teenagers but should not be undertaken by parents with younger children. It is far too long, and, with some relatively difficult ground to cover, including exposure, is best avoided by families. However, the delights of Ennerdale may still be experienced by exploring the western fringes of the lake. This is best achieved by walking around part of the bulge at this end of the lake; use one of the several carparks located further to the NE than the one suggested for the walk as the starting point and enjoy a lazy day spent by the lakeshore letting other walkers pass by.

44

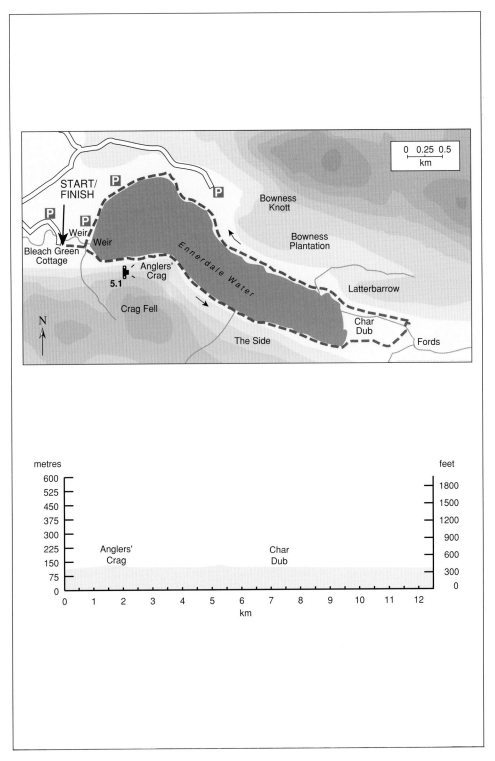

START/
FINISH

Bowness
Knott

Bowness
Plantation

Weir

Weir

Bleach Green
Cottage

Anglers'
Crag

5.1

Ennerdale Water

Latterbarrow

Crag Fell

Char
Dub

Fords

The Side

N

0 0.25 0.5
km

metres   feet

600   1800
525
450   1500
375   1200
300   900
225   Anglers'   Char   600
150   Crag   Dub
75   300
0   0

0   1   2   3   4   5   6   7   8   9   10   11   12
km

DEDICATED FELL WALKERS

Due to the remoteness of Ennerdale and the relative difficulty of getting there, this is a route with strong appeal for accomplished walkers. Alternatively, if you have sufficient time (and speed) you may prefer to continue further up the valley using the maze of paths, trails and forest roads running parallel to the River Liza to penetrate much further into Ennerdale, perhaps even as far as Black Sail Hut. This will roughly double the walking distance.

APART from residents or those holidaying in the western approaches to Ennerdale, reaching and returning from the starting part of this walk will entail a fairly lengthy road journey. From the central Lake District, be prepared to allocate at least three hours for the two car rides, so plan these as integral parts of your overall itinerary, to be enjoyed in their own right. If possible, save this trip for a fine day.

Turn L out of the carpark and cross the meandering River Ehen by means of the road bridge. After this, turn L again to walk through the recently extended carparking area, crossing over a cattle grid. Continue along the gravel path to pass through an exceptionally high K-gate and walk E along a wide unmade road down to Ennerdale Water, directly ahead. The lake provides drinking water and for some considerable time waterboard construction work (Ennerdale Weir replacement) has been in progress at the W end of the lake. Until this is finally completed you will probably be faced with a changing pattern of minor diversions, usually to the R, before reaching the water's edge.

When you do arrive at the lakeshore, in clear sunny weather you will be rewarded with the most superb views across the tranquil waters of Ennerdale. These include double-takes of the surrounding mountains faithfully reflected on the lake's motionless, mirror-like surface. These reflections will include Bowness Knott and Great Borne, both to the NE, and then to the R, of these peaks, Starling Dodd beyond leads your eye towards Red Pike and High Stile, two of the mighty fells located on the northern flank of the valley, towards its head. To the E, on your side of the water, the craggy shape of the more modest-sized Anglers' Crag rears up out of the lake, for the time being blocking out more distant views in that direction. However, you will soon be walking over this spur, when much more will be revealed.

A wooden footbridge spans a small beck and beyond this a clearly defined path winds E and then SE around the lakeshore, providing continuous views across the water and into the distant jaws of upper Ennerdale. A K-gate is negotiated, and then a grassy path leads along the rocky shore towards the rising slopes of Anglers' Crag protruding out into the dark waters below. The surrounding open scenery is a wild, remote mountainous landscape of quite exceptional rugged beauty.

The way becomes stony as it edges towards the shore and for some distance follows the bays, indents and protrusions of the lakeside. You then round the rocky bulge below the summit of Anglers' Crag. This is a wild place, characterized by boulders and scree, the debris from past rockfalls. Past these fragments, the route threads a secure way up and over the steep, rocky buttresses which form the N faces of the crag. When necessary, use your hands to steady your progress across the more difficult and exposed parts, taking your time to get up and around them.

New vistas of upper Ennerdale appear from the topmost point of this scramble around Anglers' Crag. In clear weather these extended views will include the peaks of Pillar and Steeple, both rising far away to the SE. Do make sure that your feet are anchored firmly while you take in the views, and when you do move tread with care, particularly when crossing the loose stones and shale which in places forms the relatively unstable, surface layer of the path. Following an undulation, the route obligingly drops to just above the level of the lake again, passing through dense bracken on the way down.

The path then leads through a strip of deciduous woodland, predominantly of silver birch but also containing ash, hawthorn, oak and rowan. These woods, 'The Side', are accessed by means of a P-stile in a dry stone wall.

5.1 Approaching Anglers' Crag, Ennerdale Water.

You will cross a watercourse among the trees and pass a further succession of sheltered bays and rocky beaches. Beyond these features, another small stream is crossed by 'walking the plank', after which the way leads to a P-stile positioned in a wire fence. This is the boundary line of the National Trust woodland.

Clamber over another P-stile, this one positioned near a wooden gate, and walk along a refurbished section of path to round the SE tip of Ennerdale Water. A broad, grassy path then winds through bracken from the end of the lake, leading further E up the valley. The route heads towards an extensive plantation of conifers, across another plank bridge spanning a beck. The path then skirts to the L of, firstly, larch and firs, and, further on, a rarer group of red oak with their distinctive broad leaves. When you reach a stile, climb over it and bear R to walk obediently beside the fence, as requested. This is a grassy path which in turn leads to an L-stile. Over this obstacle, cross the lane, go through a pair of gates, turn L along the forest road and within a very short distance turn L again to cross another stile, this one positioned near sheep pens.

From the sheep enclosures, head on a NE diagonal across the adjacent meadow, using the blue-circled marker posts as your main guiding line. These posts mark part of the Forestry Commission's Nine Becks Walk through Ennerdale. The way crosses the wide, flat valley bottom, and towards the far side it bends L to reach a raised footbridge over the powerful River Liza which flows down Ennerdale. Fork L on the far side of the river and follow the grassy path which leads towards the forestry road just above. The connection is made by climbing over another stile and then walking up a bracken-covered slope along a rough, stony path.

Bear L along the surfaced road to begin your return journey, then head W down the valley and pass through more forested areas, predominantly of beech with conifer plantations above. The path leads gently downhill back towards the lake, and further on you can use the more pleasant path that threads between the forest road and the River Liza. The route continues beside Char Dub and the surrounding marshy ground back to the E end of Ennerdale Water. A modest rise is encountered as the path passes through a gap in a dry stone wall and this leads to another indented section of shoreline with numerous bays and secluded stone and shingle beaches. To add to the attraction, a picnic spot is reached resplendent with a wooden table and benches.

The forest road is rejoined as further progress is made down Ennerdale. You then cross a stream as the way bisects an area of silver birch. Beyond this, more picnic spots are strategically positioned for your use. Then, just past a green-blue-and red-ringed marker post, bear off L along a side path which tracks closer to the lake. This is surfaced with chippings and leads around a brightly coloured headland which is smothered in competing bracken, gorse and heathers. This path leads just below the knobbly crag of Bowness Knott, which rises precipitously to your R. Keep L along here, following the path that skirts above the lake and ignoring alternative ways off to the R - except perhaps another picnic spot!

The relatively rough but very interesting continuation way crosses more rocky outcrops smothered in the same mixture of vegetation as before but with the added attraction of a sprinkling of rowan trees. Once again, watch where you are placing your feet in the more exposed places. Around the rocky outcrop, the path drops down to just above the waterline again, to pass by more sweeping, stony beaches. This leads to a P-stile at a wooden gate, and over this a dead-flat path, almost a promenade, continues to circle the lake in a broad arc around the sweeping NW bulge of Ennerdale Water, where the lake is at its widest.

Cross a beck feeding the lake by a wooden footbridge, which will bring you to a point where you temporarily part company with the water. Here (MR 101162), a stony path leads slightly uphill between trees to the N. A L turn over a P-stile and then a K-gate during a gradual descent will bring you back to the shoreline. The route then passes by a large, grassy carparking area, where you branch L away from the access road to these facilities. More gates, kissing and spiky, follow and then, beyond an area of tufted grasses and around the tip of a group of trees, the obvious way leads back to the River Ehen, the exit stream from Ennerdale Water. Cross the river by the bridge, turn sharp R and from here retrace your initial outward steps back to the carpark.

PLACES AND ACTIVITIES OF INTEREST

ENNERDALE AND ENNERDALE WATER

This delightful valley and lake link the lowlands surrounding Ennerdale Bridge with the mighty western fells and ridges rising to High Stile and Pillar. Extensive areas of the valley are owned by the Forestry Commission, who in more recent years have not only opened up much of their land to the public but have provided a comprehensive network of well-signed, connecting forest trails, information points and leaflets.

ANGLERS' CRAG

Anglers' Crag is the lower, rocky promontory jutting out into Ennerdale Water and is part of the much higher ground of Crag Fell which rises to 523m (1715ft). The Crag is located above the S shores of the lake towards its western end, and the walk crosses over it.

6 WASDALE HEAD AND STYHEAD TARN

STARTING/ FINISHING POINT
Carparking area at Wasdale Head
OLM 6: MR 187087

GRADING OF WALK
Moderate/ challenging

TIME ALLOWANCE
4 hours

DISTANCE
8.4km (5.2 miles)

TOTAL HEIGHT GAINED
460m (1510ft)

HIGHEST POINT
Sty Head
495m (1625ft)

GRADIENTS
The walk begins with a long, gradual pull up from the head of Wasdale, and there are some steeper sections up craggy protrusions. After this it is all downhill

PARKING
The large parking area on a grassy triangle is extremely popular, especially at weekends and on bank holidays. There are public toilets at the inn just up the valley

PUBLIC TRANSPORT
Not on a bus route

GENERAL
Most of the paths are fairly clearly defined. There are some rough, rocky sections with loose stones, but no significant challenges

TACKLING THE WALK

CASUAL WALKERS
The route is perfectly suitable for average walkers who like to be among the high fells. It is by no means too strenuous for those who are reasonably fit and should be enjoyed by anyone who is not apprehensive about venturing into rough, craggy terrain, provided this is always along recognized footpaths and the weather is favourable. The rewards for completing the route are tremendous and the advice is to try it, and if and when you have had enough on the way up simply turn around and descend back into the valley before you reach a point of 'no return'.

FAMILY WALKERS
Similar remarks to those for average walkers apply to families with older, sturdy youngsters. However, the complete route is certainly not one for younger children or for those with a nervous disposition. The latter group could spend more time exploring the delights around Wasdale Head and then, if you fancy it, walk some

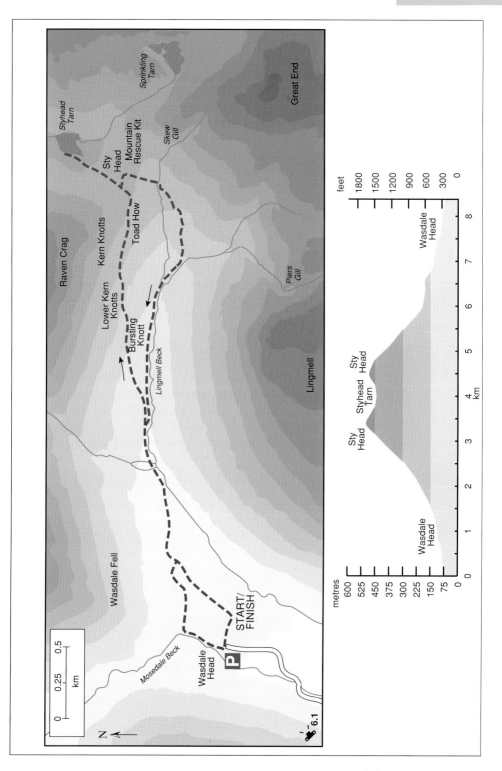

way along the lower part of Lingmell Beck, ascending above the flat valley bottom to catch some of the fine views visible towards Wast Water.

DEDICATED FELL WALKERS

Wasdale Head and its environs will almost certainly be well known to dedicated walkers. In one way or another the suggested walk will probably have formed part of more than one strenuous exploration previously undertaken *en route* to the Gables and/or Scafells. If this is not the case, it will probably already be high on your list of priorities.

WASDALE Head is a wild, remote and dramatic spot and a perfect launching pad for this challenging short walk among the high fells. Due to these desirable features it is also a difficult place to get to, although the starting point can be reached and the walk completed within a day from most locations within the Lake District, apart perhaps from the E areas.

The walk begins among magnificent mountain scenery and, almost before you take a step, the following dominant peaks may be located in clear weather: Yewbarrow (WSW), Pillar (NW), Kirk Fell (NNE), Great Gable (NE), Lingmell (ESE) and Scafell Pike (SE). Most of these mighty fells will be in view continuously for the rest of the walk, and to complete the panorama the screes of Whin Rigg and Illgill Head may be observed to the SW, dropping precipitously towards the dark, inky void of Wast Water below.

Leave the parking area along the narrow, walled lane which leads northwards towards the famed Wasdale Head Inn and the other buildings, which include The Barn Door Shop – a superior and well-stocked outdoor clothing and equipment outlet. Turn L to pass the shop, which is followed by Ritson's Bar and the public toilets (not necessarily listed in order of priority!). Then turn R to walk along the R bank of Mosedale Beck and, after crossing a P-stile, pass by the ancient pack-horse bridge but do not be tempted to cross it. Instead, continue along the wide grassy path which bends around to the R, tracking the course of the stream.

A stonier section of the route then leads gently uphill, at which point you must be careful to branch R along a narrower path which immediately bends further R still. A pleasant enclosed, grassy way then leads W up the valley criss-crossing Fogmire Beck several times by a series of five wooden bridges, the last one railed. The route leads past tree-protected Burnthwaite Farm, off to your R (excellent overnight accommodation is available here). Branch L ahead to pass through a K-gate and then cross a tributary beck by a wooden footbridge. You now reach wilder terrain where the going underfoot becomes progressively rougher, but always up a firm, secure and obvious path. During this section, the massive craggy slopes of Great Gable, Lingmell and the Scafells increasingly dominate the immediate surroundings, effectively blocking out any more distant views with their awe-inspiring combination of rock buttresses, boulders, stones, scree and tumbling watercourses.

Carry on heading E up the valley, following the winding, narrow path which threads above Lingmell Beck, a ribbon of milky water cascading down over its boulder-strewn bed and generating a great deal of noise in the process. The views back down the narrowing valley towards the fullness of Wasdale are fantastic. The way leads with great certainty towards the top of Sty Head Pass, where it intersects the path connecting Great Gable and Esk Hause at MR 219095. There are places where some easy scrambling is necessary on the way up, but this is little more than the odd steadying handhold. The imposing cliff faces, rocky spurs and buttresses, scree slopes, gullies and cascading waters along here are the breathtaking handiwork of glacial sculpturing and thousands of years of subsequent weathering. To complete the spectacle, the coast is visible from here in clear weather.

Cross over a drainage channel to reach a giant cairn, after which you will pass several more of these helpful guiding markers ahead. Towards the top of the pass the route threads between Kern Knotts, Bursting Knott and Toad How. The rock pitches of Kern Knotts are a paradise for climbers, and if you look intently to these rock pitches on your L you may spot them scaling the challenging climbing routes towering above you. Over on your R is the irregular scar of Piers Gill, ripping into the steep, inhospitable slopes between Scafell Pike, Lingmell and Broad Crag.

When you reach flatter ground continue NE over the hause, skirting the boggier ground to your R, and then descend the short distance along a gravel path to reach the sheltered shores of Styhead Tarn. Your route passes by the strategically positioned large first aid box (Mountain Rescue Post). This is a great spot to have lunch, particularly on warm, windless, sunny days. Most of the scenery in view from here has already been mentioned but beyond the tarn and Borrowdale, looking NNE through the narrow gap, are the splendid arêtes of Blencathra (Saddleback) snaking up to its wide summit area. There are also more revealing perspectives of Great Gable to the NW, with the fault line of Aaron Slack rising to Windy Gap, the hause separating Green Gable from its more famous, bigger brother. To the NE, successions of craggy slopes lead towards Glaramara, while to the SE the dark, often sunless slopes are those of Great End, with the Scafells beyond.

*6.1 Early morning
in Wasdale.*

When you have rested and eaten, retrace your outward steps the short distance uphill to the Mountain Rescue Post, walking SW to reach this spot again. Turn full L here to walk SE along the rocky path, which heads over craggy outcrops towards Esk Hause above. However, you only make use of this path for a short distance, along a fairly flat section, before branching off R along a faint grassy path which you must be vigilant to spot. This important turning is just after passing another modest marker cairn. Your changed direction is to the SW again, in line with the deep cleft of Piers Gill tearing up the craggy fellsides in front of Lingmell. Your route becomes stonier as it tracks round to the L beneath formidable rock pitches falling down towards the valley below. Following this, a rough, rocky, zigzag path leads fairly steadily downhill.

Keep above and to the L of waterlogged ground and then, near to the next cairn located on a rocky outcrop and immediately after crossing a small beck, be careful to turn R before continuing further downhill along a faint grassy path. This is instead of continuing along a branch of the better-defined and much more famous Corridor Route, which involves a tortuous ascent to the very top of England, the summit of Scafell Pike at 978m (3210ft). Your way down is much less exacting, although still indistinct in places, and it now becomes heavily cairned as it tracks W towards Wasdale, still an appreciable distance below. Fortunately, the definition of this path does improve lower down.

Another tributary beck is now crossed, and a short distance further on more steep, rocky zigzags alternate with less exacting sections of descent, before a grassy approach leads to the crossing of another beck, with a grassy track continuing beyond. The descent then leads down to and along a craggy spur, which separates two converging watercourses. Be careful to turn R before you reach the tip of this, and continue along a rocky path which crosses a stream below. This spot is marked by a small cairn and you will have to hop across the boulders conveniently positioned in the beck.

Turn L on the far side of the watercourse to continue your progress down the dale along a winding, boulder-strewn path. The rough path leads further downhill following the course of Lingmell Beck, now a formidable torrent, crossing more tributary watercourses which progressively swell the main stream. The way passes below two feathery larch trees to reach a gate in an exceptionally high, dry stone wall. Beyond this, continue down the valley along a now good, clear path to reconnect some distance further on with your outward route up the valley. Bear L along this and follow it back as far as Burnthwaite Farm. However, instead of bearing R at the end of the buildings, turn through the last gate in the wall on your L to continue down the valley along a different route.

An enclosed lane then leads towards Wasdale Head. Continue along this until you reach the tiny church of St Olaf's, and then turn R through the K-gate. You will observe a most appropriate message here, taken from Psalm 121: 'I will lift up mine eyes to the hills'. The interior of the church is well worth a visit. Afterwards, continue along the grassy path, heading W to arrive back at the tiny hamlet of Wasdale Head, reached through another K-gate. Turn L to complete the remaining short distance down the lane and back to the carparking area.

PLACES AND ACTIVITIES OF INTEREST

WASDALE HEAD
Wasdale head is a quite magnificent, wild and secluded spot positioned to the NE of Wast Water, and is the place from which it is reputed rock climbing in the Lake District first became established. Although only a tiny hamlet, it has a church, an upmarket hotel, a well-stocked outdoor leisure and equipment shop and, at nearby Burnthwaite Farm, some of the best accommodation for walkers to be found anywhere in the Lakes. It is also the perfect starting point for walking and climbing explorations into the surrounding high, challenging fells, of which there are many. It is always a most welcome haven to which to return.

STYHEAD TARN
Styhead Tarn is located at an altitude of 436m (1430ft) just below the top of the nearby pass over the hause. It occupies a superb position in a scooped-out shallow basin, partially dammed by glacial deposits, within the surrounding high fells. Among these, the steep, craggy slopes of the Gables, Great End and Seathwaite Fell sweep down to embrace it in a vice-like grip, which temporarily traps some of the catchment waters falling down these slopes. Its marshy surrounds hold no great attraction, but the easily accessible western shoreline provides relative shelter for walkers venturing into this potentially hostile environment in bad weather. It is a peaceful spot in which to recharge your batteries before more exertions among the fells. The tarn's maximum depth is about 10m (30ft) and small trout are said to inhabit its waters.

7 RAVENGLASS & ESKDALE RAILWAY AND MUNCASTER FELL

**STARTING/
FINISHING POINT**
Dalegarth station
carpark OLM 6: MR
173007. Walk starts
at Muncaster Mill
(MR 096977) and
finishes at The
Green Station
(MR 145998)

**GRADING OF
WALK**
Easy/
straightforward

TIME ALLOWANCE
3 hours

DISTANCE
7.3km (4.5 miles)

**TOTAL
HEIGHT GAINED**
250m (820ft)

HIGHEST POINT
Muncaster Fell
231m (760ft)

GRADIENTS

The walk starts with a steep climb through woodland, followed by longer, more gradual ascent of Muncaster Fell, which steepens again near the top. The rest of the route is either flat or downhill, apart from a few minor undulations

PARKING

Large, attractively screened carpark beside Whillan Beck

PUBLIC TRANSPORT

Not on a bus route

GENERAL

With few exceptions, the paths are reasonable to very good, although there may be some wet and boggy patches following heavy rain

TACKLING THE WALK

CASUAL WALKERS

This is a walk that the great majority of casual walkers should really enjoy. It has a few relatively demanding uphill sections, but these are interspersed with easier parts and the route – particularly in fine weather – is well within the capabilities of anyone who is reasonably fit. One of the rewards is the magnificent views from the top of Muncaster Fell.

FAMILY WALKERS

The entire walk is suitable for families, providing the children are able to walking about 8km (5 miles) or so across open fellsides and are suitably attired. Fine, clear and preferably warm weather should be certain before the walk is attempted by families. Those with younger children, perhaps below the age of eight or nine, are advised to spend the day around Muncaster Castle, perhaps walking along part of the coast and returning by train from Ravenglass.

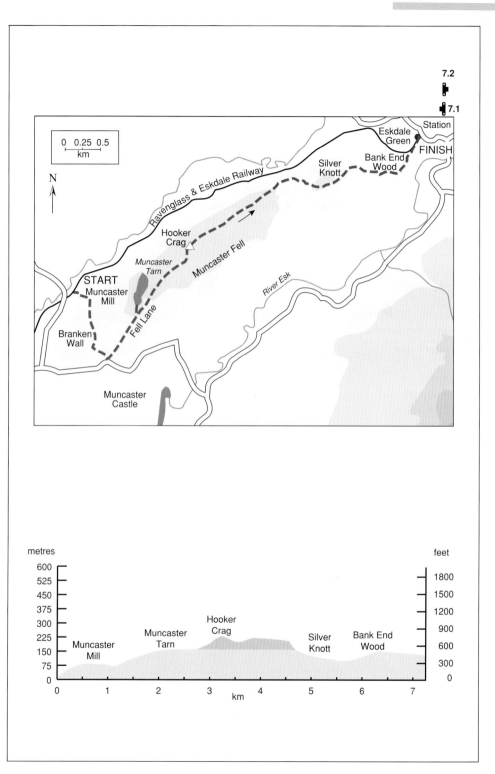

7.2

7.1

Station

Eskdale
Green

FINISH

Ravenglass & Eskdale Railway

Silver
Knott

Bank End
Wood

Hooker
Crag

*Muncaster
Tarn*

Muncaster Fell

START
Muncaster
Mill

River Esk

Branken
Wall

Fell Lane

Muncaster
Castle

0   0.25 0.5
km

N

metres

feet

600
525
450
375
300
225
150
75
0

1800

1500

1200

900

600

300

0

Hooker
Crag

Muncaster
Tarn

Silver
Knott

Bank End
Wood

Muncaster
Mill

0   1   2   3   4   5   6   7
km

DEDICATED FELL WALKERS

A walk over Muncaster Fell should appeal to any keen walker, and the stronger ones may prefer to dispense with the supporting train journeys. An itinerary which may suit the very fittest is to walk around Mediobogdum Roman Fort, take a stroll through Boot and around Blea Tarn, and save Muncaster Fell until after breakfast!

THIS walk begins first with a train journey of just over half an hour from Dalegarth station to Muncaster Mill, and you will need to plan your itinerary according to which attractions you wish to visit and the scheduled train times. The return journey is from The Green station back to Dalegarth. When you board for the outward trip, you must alert the guard that you wish to alight at the mill, because this is a request stop only. The train journey covers just 10km (6 miles) and passes through a succession of cuttings and beneath bridges along the interesting wooded valley of Eskdale and around the northern flank of Muncaster Fell, to arrive at Muncaster Mill for the start of the walk. Unless you intend to spend some time looking around the fascinating mill with its huge water wheel, walk right through the mill yard past an entrance where tickets are demanded (you are in fact on a public right of way).

7.1 A colourful corner of Boot.

Bear R at the end of the mill yard along the signed bridleway, to connect with a broad track above. Turn R along this, following the way signed to Castle and Ravenglass, but within a few paces be careful to turn L along a path signed 'Bridleway – Castle'. A steep slope stretches ahead and this is scaled along a stony path which heads E. It is quite a pull up, so take your time and select a pace which is comfortable for the entire party. The ascent is through enclosed, mixed woodland, but when you reach the edge of more open terrain and the steeper gradient relents, bear R along a connecting path to continue S, guided by a broad, grassy track. This excellent way leads through a wide gap in an area of attractive and more open woodland, before gradually descending in the direction of Muncaster Castle. Keep to the main permitted path down through the woods, ignoring a bridleway off to your R. The correct way leads to a five-barred gate at Branken Wall. Go through it and turn L, then follow the wide gravel track down to the A595(T), reaching this road at MR 101968, opposite the grounds of Muncaster Castle.

Proceed through the gateway at the road and then turn immediately L to continue up the public bridleway signed Muncaster Fell via Fell Lane. From here a wide track leads gently uphill past clusters of blackberry bushes, the fruits of which are usually ripe for plundering in September. Beyond a gate, the first good clear views of the surrounding countryside begin to emerge. The best of these are to the SE through gaps in the surrounding foliage, the vast, rolling uplands rising towards Whitfell. After an iron gate, keep walking up the slope along the firm, clear, grassy track which continues the traverse NE. The way then undulates downhill, equally gently.

The path leads NE through the fringe of the woodlands, and higher up you should keep straight on along the public footpath signed to Eskdale instead of turning R along the bridleway leading towards lower Eskdale. A K-gate ahead marks the boundary of more open countryside, and from hereabouts there is the thrill of spotting the summit of Muncaster Fell, your next major objective. This peak is straight ahead above the more immediate foreground of gorse and rhododendron bushes. Bear L along the track heading most directly towards the visible triangulation point at the top of the fell, skirting around a plantation of pines to your L in order to do so.

The final approach to the summit of Muncaster Fell is up steeper, rougher ground over exposed pink granite, but in fine, clear weather the all-round panoramas from this isolated vantage point are simply breathtaking. The landscapes in view from here are vast and include a fair stretch of coastline together with the adjacent flat strip of land around Ravenglass, both of these to the W.

Now rotate slowly through 180°, allowing your eyes to track along Eskdale and the other valleys which penetrate into these western-most high fells, and feast upon the mountain masterpiece which includes Pillar (NNE), Kirk Fell and the Scafells (NE), Bow Fell and Crinkle Crags (ENE), Harter and Ulpha Fells (E), and part of the Coniston Fells, also to the E.

Descend to the E, following the grassy path which tracks along the higher ground of the undulating ridge for some distance. The descent is initially down a fairly steep section, but this will soon be behind you. Ahead, branch R and keep to the more obvious way – do not become confused by misleading sheep tracks. Your direction remains towards the E and this is your main guiding beacon. Higher, rockier ground is passed to your L, but be careful not to lose any significant height just yet, achieving this by climbing up the grassy brow ahead. After this you will cross more undulating ground and begin to appreciate the massive scale of this fell, with its many bumps and hollows secreted within the extensive SW–NE crest.

A steeper slope, covered with heather and bracken, then leads down to a wider path below. Turn L along this and prepare for the boggier, wetter ground that lies ahead. There are several alternative mini ways through this section but, providing you do not stray from a dominant E to NE diagonal which holds the higher ground, it matters very little which one you select. Beyond the wet patches, a dry, grassy track will lead you through a gap in a dry stone wall. From here the route is virtually all downhill, along a peaty way directly towards Eskdale below.

The clear, obvious descent loses height gradually, always snaking further eastwards and circling around another craggy, bracken- and heather-clad hillock in the process. This is the knobbly shape of Silver Knott. Some more marginal climbing is involved ahead, before another path merges with yours and the combined way then leads further downhill along a series of fairly straight traverses. The descent leads through a K-gate (tight squeeze!) and then an extensive gorse thicket, and more height is lost as the path continues down through more glorious mud. Your direction remains towards the E.

The route leads to an intersection of paths below, at MR 139993. Pass over the P-stile adjacent to the metal gate and then follow the way leading directly ahead, which is helpfully signed 'Bridleway – The Green and Station'. The bridleway leads NE across open meadowland. When you reach another usually muddy area ahead located near a group of trees covering a rocky knoll, you should veer L. This will lead you beside a stone wall, which you follow as it bears further L at the edge of more fields, to deposit you eventually in a dell surrounded by trees. These trees are part of

Bankend Wood. Cross over the small beck and then use the stile near a wooden gate. After this, a stony path leads beneath more trees and then beside the railway line, to bring you to The Green station – with luck, at a time convenient for catching the next train back to Dalegarth.

7.2 Eskdale with a section of the 'Ratty' near Dalegarth.

PLACES AND ACTIVITIES OF INTEREST

RAVENGLASS & ESKDALE RAILWAY

The 'La'al Ratty' as it is affectionately known, was opened in 1875 to transport iron ore from local mines to the main Furnace Railway along the coast. It started carrying passengers the following year. Since then the railway has had an unsettled history, but due to the efforts of enthusiasts, later on supported by members of the Preservation Society, the once nearly derelict line has been refurbished and is now one of the major tourist attractions in the north-west of England. The line now operates between Dalegarth in Eskdale and Ravenglass on the coast. This is a journey of about 11 km (7 miles) and takes some 40 minutes, the train stopping (when travelling down the valley) at Beckfoot, The Green, Irton Road, Muncaster Mill and Ravenglass stations. This trip is promoted as the most beautiful train journey in England. The train schedules operate in seasonal bands, with the most frequent services during the main holiday periods.

For further details, including party rates, or to obtain a brochure and timetable, contact the Ravenglass & Eskdale Railway Co Ltd. (see Useful Addresses).

63

MUNCASTER MILL

Take a step back in time when you alight from the train at Muncaster Mill to visit a working, water-powered flour mill where organic flour is milled daily. The mill has been restored by The Eskdale (Cumbria) Trust.

MUNCASTER CASTLE

For further information, special events, opening times and so on, contact Muncaster Castle (see Useful Addresses, contact telephone numbers).

Muncaster Castle dominates the River Esk and has been of strategic importance since Roman times. The view from its terrace has been described as the 'gateway to paradise', and the castle and extensive grounds are now a major tourist attraction. Apart from the absorbing tour of the castle treasures, there are extensive gardens containing a superb collection of rhododendrons and other exotic trees and shrubs, an owl centre, a nature trail, a wildfowl pond, a children's play area, a refreshment buttery and a gift shop.

ESKDALE CORN MILL

For further information contact the helpful mill manager David King (see Useful Addresses).

A short walk away from Dalegarth station, Eskdale Corn Mill located at Boot is one of the very few surviving two-wheel water corn mills. It dates back to 1578, but this is long after milling first came to Eskdale in the twelfth century. Visitors will be able to enjoy a fascinating exhibition explaining the milling process and the workings of the unique wooden machinery. As a treat, look for the extremely rare royal fern growing near the water pool.

MEDIOBOGDUM ROMAN FORT

This site of historical importance is now under the care of the National Trust, from whom further information may be obtained (see Useful Addresses).

Built on a windswept hillside to withstand the elements and survive for centuries, the Roman Fort commanding Hardknott Pass has done just this. This square fort from the first century AD is magnificently preserved and was built in the reign of Hadrian (118–138) to be garrisoned by the fourth Cohort of Dalmations as protection for important trade route over the pass. Its extensive buildings were constructed of stone and timber and included such refinements as main buildings, headquarters, a commandant's house, storerooms, barracks, and a bath house which contained cold, changing, warm, and hot rooms.

THE LANGDALE VALLEYS

8 AROUND BLEA TARN

**STARTING/
FINISHING POINT**
Carpark adjacent to
the minor road near
Blea Tarn
OLM 6: MR 296043

**GRADING OF
WALK**
Easy/
straightforward

TIME ALLOWANCE
1½ hours

DISTANCE
2.2km (1.4 miles)

**TOTAL HEIGHT
GAINED**
45m (150ft)

HIGHEST POINT
Bleatarn House
213m (700ft)

GRADIENTS
The route is virtually flat

PARKING
The small carpark for the tarn has been extended to hold 15–20 cars, and is very popular

PUBLIC TRANSPORT
Not on a bus route (a local service is planned)

GENERAL
The paths to and around the tarn are excellent, while those in the northern loop are narrower, less clear and include some wet patches. There is convenient wheelchair access to the tarn

TACKLING THE WALK

CASUAL WALKERS
The route is almost perfectly sculpted for less ambitious walkers. It requires modest effort, has no appreciable uphill bits and the surroundings and views are continuously magnificent! Complete the walk on a fine, sunny day and you will certainly want to return.

FAMILY WALKERS
Similar remarks apply to family groups as to casual walkers. The walk down to and around the western shores of the tarn is particularly popular with young families, and children will certainly enjoy playing around at the water's edge.

DEDICATED FELL WALKERS
This walk will probably be completed quite naturally as an integral part of a longer route into the higher fells, perhaps *en route* to Pike of Blisco and points above, further W. However, it makes a fine, short leg-stretch when motoring over Wrynose and Hardknott Passes, and is also a delightful evening stroll aimed at capturing a

Previous page:
Colwith Force.

66

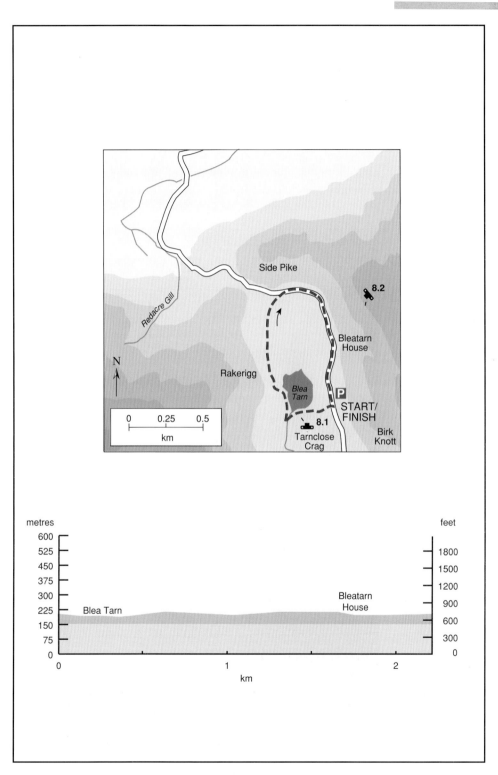

particularly promising sunset or to combine with a more energetic climb on to Lingmoor Fell.

THE setting for this short walk – a secluded, elevated shelf among the high fells – is absolutely superb, particularly on crisp, sunny days in either the early morning or late evening. From the carpark, cross over the minor road and pass through the K-gate opposite to enter the National Trust land in which Blea Tarn is located. The surrounding scenery is terrific, with high, craggy fells rearing up in all directions. The sprawling starfish shape of Wetherlam occupies the SSW across Little Langdale Valley, the

craggy bulk of Rakerigg sweeps up directly ahead beyond the tarn, the skyline of the Langdale Pikes rises triumphantly to the NNW, the precipitous crag of the closer Side Pike juts up to the N, and behind you are the westerly slopes of Lingmoor Fell – what a panorama, and you have not yet ventured more than a few paces!

This magnificent array of surrounding mountains is mellowed somewhat by the contrasting sheltered, still waters of Blea Tarn which, when there is the slightest sunshine about, shimmer ahead down to your R. This serene scene is enhanced by the fringing coppice of conifers, mainly Scots pine and spruce, together with rhododendron bushes.

8.1 Early morning reflections in Blea Tarn.

Follow the refurbished wide, dry path down to the southern tip of the tarn, descending gently to the W. The path snakes to bring you to a K-gate through which you pass at the tip of the tarn. From here, the path curves L to cross Bleamoss Beck, the exit stream from the tarn. However, before you reach the stream you will pass a wooden bench to your R and from this position there is one of the finest views of the Langdale Pikes to be observed from any compass point. This is across the tarn, with the overhanging branches of a group of feathery larch trees providing a photogenic framing of the Pikes, and on still days the unbroken surface waters of the tarn supply the mirror necessary for producing perfect reflections of these fells.

There is a wooden footbridge over the stream and on the far side of this you should select the first branch path leading off to the R, the one nearest to the edge of the tarn. This will lead you norhtwards around the tarn. The way then winds through rhododendron bushes and, further on, under the cooling shade of larch and Scots pine, never venturing far away from the inviting shores of the tarn down on your R. These provide numerous sheltered picnic spots frequently occupied by family groups during hot, balmy days in summer. The path then bears L up a shallow gradient as it circles around a small, wooded spur jutting out into the tarn.

8.2 Blea Tarn and the snow-topped peaks of Wetherlam and Swirl How.

70

You leave the immediate, wooded surrounds of Blea Tarn through another K-gate, after which the path, although still wide and distinct, becomes rougher as its surface changes to compacted stone and protruding rock fragments. The way continues quite gradually uphill from here, with a combination wire fence and dry stone wall on your R. In this section you will pass a solitary spruce tree nearby. Further on, veer R across tufted grass to reconnect with the wire fence/dry stone wall combination, and then follow it northwards until you reach a P-stile over a rusty wire fence straight ahead (be careful here, because the supporting post may be loose). On the far side, follow the course of the now somewhat dilapidated stone wall, keeping this near to you on your R. In wet conditions, you will need to cross some patches of clinging, boggy ground, or avoid them by small detours.

The way now curves around gracefully to the R and rises to connect with the minor road at MR 292051, where an s-stile is located to your L. Turn R along the lane and use this to return to the carpark about 1km (½ mile) away. In doing so, be ever vigilant about approaching traffic, particularly if you have young children with you, as there are several blind bends where you need to observe with your ears rather than your eyes. You will pass the pleasantly situated Bleatarn House *en route*, which provides bed and breakfast. After this, there is a short pull up the slope ahead and a few more downhill bends before you arrive back at the carpark. Just before you reach your vehicle, look R over the dry stone wall, where in fine weather there is a glimpse of Crinkle Crags together with the proud peak of Bow Fell to the WNW.

PLACES AND ACTIVITIES OF INTEREST

BLEA TARN

This is a small, natural tarn filling a shallow basin in a shelf perched between and above Great and Little Langdale Valleys. It is situated at 185m (600ft) above sea level and has a maximum depth of under 10m (30ft). With its surrounding amphitheatre of high craggy fells, its sheltered position, and its rocky western shoreline covered by rhododendron, larch and Scots pine, it is a popular spot with walkers and picnickers alike, particularly during summer school holidays. The access paths have recently been upgraded and there is now a convenient wheelchair approach to the tarn from the nearby carpark. Perch, pike and brown trout are said to inhabit the clear waters.

9 ELTERWATER, SKELWITH FORCE, COLWITH FORCE AND SLATER BRIDGE

**STARTING/
FINISHING POINT**
Elterwater village
green OLM 7: MR
328048

**GRADING OF
WALK**
Moderate/
challenging

TIME ALLOWANCE
3½ hours

DISTANCE
8.9 km (5.6 miles)

**TOTAL HEIGHT
GAINED**
155m (510ft)

HIGHEST POINT
Beneath Howe
Banks (during
return) 150m
(490ft)

GRADIENTS
There is a short, sharp pull up from Slater Bridge followed by a longer, more gradual ascent around Howe Banks, plus one or two other modest uphill sections

PARKING
The popular carpark near the village centre has recently been enlarged to take about 25 cars. There is an additional parking area above the village off the B5343 road

PUBLIC TRANSPORT
CMS bus route 516 Ambleside to Dungeon Ghyll (The Langdale Rambler)

GENERAL
The paths are mostly good, but with some erosion in places. The wooded areas can be wet and the valley between Elterwater and Skelwith Bridge floods after prolonged rain, so take your wellingtons

TACKLING THE WALK

CASUAL WALKERS
This is a fine, not too strenuous walk full of interesting features, and with absorbing views, both near and far. For most of the way it is a route which should appeal very much to less ambitious walkers.

FAMILY WALKERS
The route is fine for families with older children, say over the age of 10. There are places where everybody, particularly children, will need to be careful and you should bear this in mind as you approach these spots, which are identified in the route description. Families with very young children may wish to turn back at Skelwith Bridge if time is short.

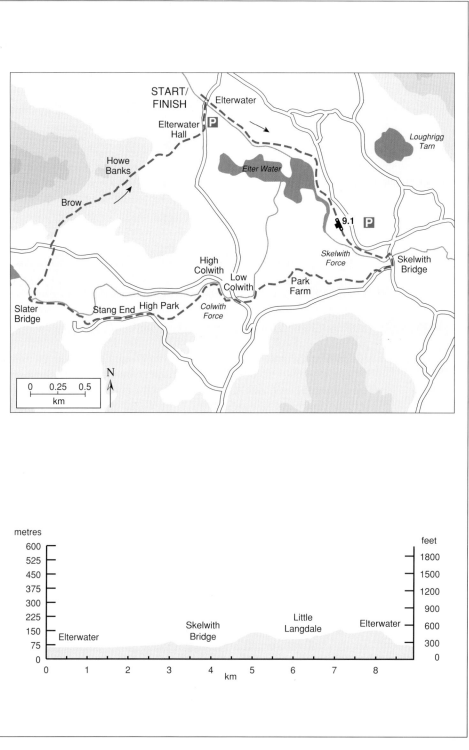

START/
FINISH

Elterwater

Elterwater
Hall

Howe
Banks

Brow

Elter Water

*Loughrigg
Tarn*

9.1

*Skelwith
Force*

Skelwith
Bridge

High
Colwith

Low
Colwith

Park
Farm

Slater
Bridge

Stang End High Park *Colwith
Force*

N

| 0 | 0.25 | 0.5 |
km

metres		feet
600		1800
525
450		1500
375		1200
300
225		900
150		600
75
0		0

Elterwater

Skelwith
Bridge

Little
Langdale

Elterwater

0   1   2   3   4   5   6   7   8
km

DEDICATED FELL WALKERS

Although this is an unchallenging, low-level walk of modest distance, there is plenty of interest and it makes a fine half-day or evening stroll. Parts of the route and many of the highlights may be incorporated into longer walks through the district, for example when descending along Great Langdale from the Pikes or Lingmoor Fell, or when coming off Wetherlam and walking the length of Little Langdale.

EAVE the attractive centre of Elterwater with its village green, specimen maple tree, white-painted Britannia Inn and Corner Tuck Shop, and walk s along the exit road signed 'Coniston 5 – Little Langdale 2½'. However, before crossing the River Brathay and still within the built-up area, turn L to cross through the National Trust carpark, following a signed public footpath. Then bear R to pass through a K-gate, keeping to the footpath signed to Skelwith Bridge. From here, a pleasant refurbished, wide path follows the course of the River Brathay downstream to the SE.

Wide views soon open up on your L across flat green meadows, with the craggy shape of the undulating band of rock which protects the N flank of Great Langdale valley. This runs in a broad sweeping arc from Blea Rigg in the W to Loughrigg Fell in the E. The level path of stone chippings continues adjacent to the attractive tree-fringed banks of the river, gurgling away just below you on the R. The first tantalizing views of Elter Water then appear ahead to the R, as you grapple with tree roots across your way and cross a wooden bridge over a side stream. At this stage, turn around to enjoy an unimpeded view of the Langdale Pikes poking up at the head of the valley to the NW. Given clear weather, the dominant peaks of Pike of Stickle, Harrison Stickle and Pavey Ark are all in view. The lower mountain to the L of these giants is Lingmoor Fell, rising more gently to the W, and there is a particularly good view of this when framed through a gap in the foliage of a nearby wizened beech tree.

The wide path bends L across another bridge, then winds back R to continue along the edge of a wooded area on your R. Shy Elter Water lies to the S, its shape mostly hidden by the foliage of the intervening trees. The shores of the lake can be reached down one of the often boggy side paths leading that way, and the reward from its reeded shores is a sighting of the northernmost slopes of Wetherlam, rising majestically as long ridges to the SW. After this minor diversion, make your way down the wooded valley, seen at its best in May when the shaded ground beneath the trees is lavishly carpeted with bluebells. Further on, be careful to keep to the lower path ignoring a side path leading off L up the grassy slopes.

You leave the wooded area at a K-gate positioned in a stone boundary wall. Wander down to the river here to obtain the most magnificent view across Elter Water back up the valley towards Lingmoor Fell and the Pikes. The route continues downstream across pleasant, tree-fringed flat meadowlands, following the meandering course of the Brathay – wellingtons may be required. More K-gates are negotiated, and the flat meadows terminate at another of these positioned at a wider gateway. Beyond this an enclosed, stony path leads through woodland to Skelwith Force, down on your R. An inspection of the cascading waters is a must, but even though the access paths to these falls have been improved you should still maintain the utmost vigilance with children while here and keep a tight hand on the younger ones.

Continue down the valley from the falls, keeping to the path between the dusty, often noisy, sheds of Kirkstone Quarry Works. Exercise care again here and be aware of the danger from the movements of forklift trucks during working hours. Just past this busy working area is the delightful Kirkstone Galleries, just off to your R. Apart from their specialist slate products, these tastefully organized showrooms offer a variety of gifts and delicious refreshments.

From the galleries, continue down to the A593 Ambleside–Coniston road and turn R along this using the arched Skelwith Bridge to cross the River Brathay. There is a nasty bend here, so watch out for fast-approaching traffic. There are also more opportunities for refreshments, including the Skelwith Bridge Hotel to the L as you approach the road and, across the river, the Rosewood Tea Gardens on your R. Walk uphill along the road to pass by Greenbank B&B, and then be careful to ignore the first narrow footpath leading off on your side of the road to the R as this circles back to the falls, where it comes to a dead end.

The route passes by Ivy Cottage with its attractive gardens, and after this bear R along the public footpath signed to Colwith Force. Access to the path is through a waymarked K-gate and this leads to the National Trust land at Bridge How Coppice. The route is now along a path of compacted earth which leads SW uphill away from the private road on your R. You then climb a moderate slope as the path winds through deciduous woodland, and negotiate two more K-gates positioned to either side of a small beck. The gradient now levels off as more open countryside is reached. Bear R at the junction of paths ahead, to continue W along the side of the shallow valley. The wide path winds around a residence named Tiplog. Follow the yellow waymarkers here, passing through two more K-gates, one modern and the other of ancient wrought iron.

A short distance further on the way passes a semi-permanent group of assorted caravans and then, following another modest incline, reaches Park Farm, dating from 1879. A signpost at this spot indicates that your direction is towards Elterwater and Colwith. Pass between the farm buildings and towards the end of these look out for a distinctive stone slab in the barn wall on your L. This contains six versions of the alphabet and is thought to be the work of an apprentice stonemason. Be careful to leave from the farmyard through a waymarked gap at the side of a stone barn, and then walk directly ahead along a path which leads further up the valley between two private driveways, one leading to the residence named Ruthwaite to your R above.

The correct route is confirmed when you reach a wooden s-stile breaching a stone wall across the path, followed by a narrow, stepped G-stile in a second wall. A more enclosed section of path leads to another stile, followed by a K-gate, before the now elevated way winds around a grassy hillock. In clear weather Wetherlam may be spotted again directly ahead, while to its R the craggy, purple profile of Pike of Blisco rises to the WNW directly above Low Colwith. Another s-stile provides entry to a belt of woodland, through which your narrow path descends steeply to the valley

9.1 Wetherlam reflected in the River Brathay.

floor below. Take care going down and use your hands to steady yourself – there are plenty of branches to grab hold of. Near the bottom, a stepped P-stile signals that the worst is over.

The route now leads to the minor lane connecting Elterwater with the main Ambleside–Coniston road, which is reached at a wall where slate steps have been embedded to assist you in climbing over (MR 331030). Turn R along the road, but within about 100 paces turn L off it up a public footpath to scale another stone wall, aided by more steps. After negotiating the adjacent P-stile, turn sharp R along the path signed to Colwith Force, thus avoiding the alternative path straight ahead which leads uphill missing the falls. The continuation way ascends a craggy slope and then leads through more woodland along a narrow but clearly defined, winding way, with the stream below on your R. Keep to the main path along here and do not be tempted along any side paths off to your L.

Follow the narrow path as it continues to wind gently uphill under a thick covering of foliage, and when it divides fork R along the continuation path nearest to the stream, which is now spasmodically in view below through gaps in the otherwise densely packed trees. The path leads to a superb viewing position overlooking Colwith Force. However, be vigilant here, particularly when you are manoeuvring to obtain the best position from which to take photographs, because there is not much room and a potentially very dangerous drop awaits the unwary. The waterfall is made up of several separate drops, the water plunging down each of these in succession through a narrow, rocky gorge, the surrounding steep, tree-covered slopes blotting out more distant views and encapsulating the viewer in solitude. The catchment pool at the bottom of the falls is popular with dippers and grey wagtails.

Continue up the steep and in places quite slippery path, exercising care towards the steep fall-away on your R, and locate one of several rough, narrow paths which merge further up and then wind through the upper reaches of the woods away from the stream and waterfalls. The continuation path threads SW under trees, including some fine specimen beech and sycamore, and across often waterlogged ground before it emerges from the shade at MR 325028, still gaining height. The path then leads to a bridleway, which runs along the edge of the woodland. Veer R down this to pass through a K-gate, now heading due W more directly up Little Langdale valley.

The route takes you into more open landscapes which, after the enclosed woodland, are particularly stimulating. The expansive view ahead takes in the attractively situated farm of High Park and beyond this an amphitheatre of high fells, including the summits of Pike of Blisco, Bow Fell and the Lingmoor Fell/Side Pike ridge, all of which are visible in clear weather. Next pass through the way-marked K-gate on your R (blue arrowhead denoting bridleway) and walk down to and between the farm buildings, entering the farm via another K-gate and leaving through a gate on your L which brings you on to a surfaced lane. Bear R along this and continue down it, ignoring the public footpath leading down off on your R. Also avoid another footpath further on, this one branching off to the L uphill, and then continue straight ahead at Stang End, ignoring yet another public footpath off to the R.

The lane then leads downhill, where you cross over a cattle grid followed by a small beck. Turn sharp R just over the bridge, abandoning the hard surface for a grassy path that threads around the wooded hillock ahead. The path leads to a wider track along which you bear R, walking beside Atkinson Coppice. Further on, do not cross the main stream by the footbridge but instead bear L along the wide track which continues to lead up the valley. The way then passes through a gateway as quarry spoils appear above to your L. As you approach the next gateway you should spot Slater Bridge, revealed on the far side of a stone wall down on your R. The path down to the attractive arched bridge is accessed through a K-gate on your R, a short distance further on.

On warm, sunny days crossing the bridge, particularly if you have either children or photographers with you, could take a long time. The setting is compelling and particularly photogenic, and the relatively adventurous way across the stream is over a stepped W-stile, across an aged, hunchbacked bridge complete with iron handrail, and finally across linking slate slabs over a second channel of water. The route continues uphill from the bridge over an outcrop of rocks to reach the higher ground of High Birk Howe, and then on to Birk Howe Farm. More superb views appear across Little Langdale Tarn as you gain height. After passing through another K-gate and then a wider gate, turn L along the approach track to the farm and use this to reach the minor road through Little Langdale at MR 314035.

Cross over the road on a diagonal to your L and then turn R along the surfaced side lane, which is signed 'Unsuitable for Vehicles'. Use this to walk further uphill, heading NE. The route then passes by Dale End Farm, and after this the going underfoot becomes rougher and in wet spells appreciably boggier. After yet another gate, the way bisects an attractive clump of gorse ahead and you should now keep to the main wide track, avoiding all diversions off to both L and R, and maintaining a NE bearing. A long, gradual descent then follows which, after passing through a final gateway, will lead you back to Elterwater. Before reaching the village, your rough, stony track connects with a surfaced lane, which in turn will guide you down to Coniston Road. Turn L along this and follow it the short distance back to the centre of Elterwater and the carparks.

PLACES AND ACTIVITIES OF INTEREST

ELTERWATER (VILLAGE) AND ELTER WATER (LAKE)
The picturesque village of Elterwater is famed for its grass triangle and maple tree, brilliant in its gold autumn foliage. The white-painted Britannia Inn and complementing Corner Post Office are a mecca for tourists and walkers alike, which unfortunately leads to an excess of cars. Access to the eggtimer-shaped, reeded lake is limited, but there is an excellent spot near its eastern end, which is also often favoured by a pair of swans.

SKELWITH FORCE (WATERFALL)
There is only a modest drop at these falls, but, due to a combination of the volume of water cascading over them, the smoothed, irregular rocks over which it tumbles and the dark, sinister catchment pool at the base, the overall effect is electrifying. Some of the best vantage spots call for minor scrambling, and the wet rocks across which this has to be performed add to the excitement and thrill of visiting the spot.

KIRKSTONE GALLERIES
See Walk 10.

COLWITH FORCE
This waterfall is different from Skelwith Force in almost every respect. Observed from a ledge some distance away from the plunging waters and spray, the whole fascinating scene is taken in at a glance. This is of a series of falls, each tumbling down a portion of a narrow, broken, rocky cleft set among the most delightful surrounding woodland.

SLATER BRIDGE
An ancient, humpbacked pack-horse (now foot) bridge spanning the outlet stream from Little Langdale Tarn, this bridge and its setting are incredibly photogenic and the silence is often shattered by the clicking of camera shutters. There are at least two explanations for its name: one that it is derived from the slate slabs from which the crossing was constructed, and the other associated with the workmen who used to cross it on their way to work in the nearby slate quarries.

10 LOUGHRIGG TARN AND SKELWITH FORCE

**STARTING/
FINISHING POINT**
Silverthwaite
National Trust
carpark OLM 7: MR
341037

**GRADING OF
WALK**
Easy/
straightforward

TIME ALLOWANCE
1½ hour

DISTANCE
3.2km (2 miles)

**TOTAL HEIGHT
GAINED**
45m (150ft)

HIGHEST POINT
Crag Head
105m (345ft)

GRADIENTS
The walk starts with an easy ascent but is all downhill after this, apart
from the final easy pull up to the carpark

PARKING
Spacious carpark for 25-30 cars

PUBLIC TRANSPORT
CMS bus route 516 Ambleside to Dungeon Ghyll (The Langdale Rambler)

GENERAL
Although narrow and overgrown in places, the paths are relatively easy
to follow, with few wet areas

TACKLING THE WALK

CASUAL WALKERS
This a walk for all seasons, all weathers, and perhaps all walkers. In
any event, it is a splendid short walk; the modest climbing is soon
over and then there is delight upon delight as the route winds
downhill past a tarn, refreshment places, a waterfall and finally
along an attractive valley. Definitely one to add to your repertoire,
or to dust off if it is already there.

FAMILY WALKERS
The remarks for casual walkers apply equally to families, with the
addendum that children will love this walk as well!

DEDICATED FELL WALKERS
This short walk makes a delightful introductory evening stroll on
the first day of a weekend or longer holiday spent in the Lake
District. Alternatively, the circuit can be incorporated easily into
several longer walks in the area, routes using Loughrigg Fell or
passing over Red Bank being the obvious choice.

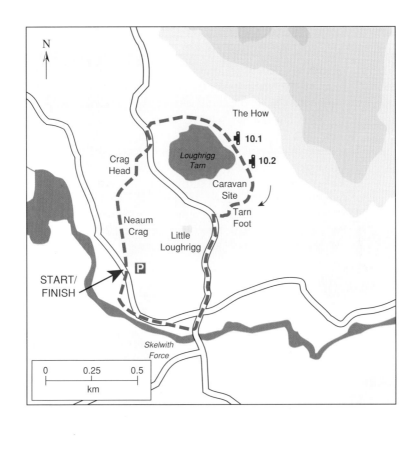

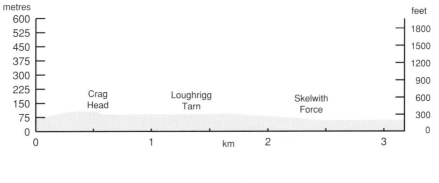

ALK back towards the entrance to the carpark and then bear R to pass through the private parking area reserved for Silverthwaite Cottage. Turn R uphill and head towards the entrance gate to the cottage. To the R of this wooden gate a narrow path winds up the fell, passing through dense bracken and beneath the shade of silver birch trees. Follow this path, almost immediately forking R up the steeper route and gaining height quickly to the N as you pass through enclosed shrubbery. Although narrow, the path is clearly defined but does tend to become obstructed by the pervading bracken, particularly in the summer.

The route passes beneath power cables and then tracks for some distance beside a stone wall on your L before the more open fellsides are reached. The path then bends L, followed by a straight-ish diagonal cutting a swathe through the bracken-covered slopes, and continues to gain height as it passes beneath a more substantial power line. Open views now emerge over to your L across Great Langdale valley, including sightings of Wetherlam (WSW), Lingmoor Fell (NW) and a peep of the Langdale Pikes towards the head of the valley, their domed peaks punctuating the sky to the NNW. Your continuation path still runs N to an intersection with a broader path running at right angles to your approach. Turn R along this better-defined way, changing your direction to E, and continue climbing, now towards a V-shaped nick on the near horizon. This is positioned to the L of a clump of conifers, mostly larch.

The way up converges on a dry stone wall towards the top of the slope and the line of this will guide you the short remaining distance to reach the brow above. When you get to the shallow hause, divert from the path for a few paces to scale the craggy rock outcrops above to your L, as these vantage points provide excellent unobstructed views of the surrounding landscapes. This includes the first sighting of part of Loughrigg Fell and the magical tarn filling the basin at its base. The sheltered waters of Loughrigg Tarn are spectacular, cupped in the embrace of the surrounding folded fellsides, which are liberally sprinkled with both broadleaved and coniferous trees. Your path will shortly take you around the N and E shoreline of these placid waters, where you will be able to observe the tame waterfowl and other wildlife at close quarters. From this rocky perch there are fantastic views down into Great Langdale, where the complete egg-timer shape of Elter Water is fully revealed. Also, through a convenient gap to the N, the vast, rolling fellsides rising towards the summit of Helvellyn may be seen on clear days. One other fell of interest is the summit of Wansfell Pike, strutting up from a ridge to the E and overlooking Ambleside.

When you have seen enough of this splendid panorama, return to the path below and turn L to begin your descent towards Loughrigg Tarn. This is now not very far away, and the route is all either downhill or on the flat. Turn L again when you have completed the first short, steeper section down, turning away from an inviting S-stile to your R. From here a broad, grassy track leads N downhill and then connects with the entrance drive to a secluded stone cottage named Crag Head. Bear L along this gravel drive and use it to reach the minor road below, passing by a second white-painted cottage on the way.

Turn L along the lane, but within less than 200 paces climb over the stile on your R which provides access to a signed public footpath. This leads downhill across open meadows to Loughrigg Tarn, below on your R. Before you get there you will need to use a substantial L-stile to cross a formidable stone wall barring your approach. The stile is positioned near to a beech tree and you will need a head for heights to get over it without any qualms! After this, the rest of the way to the tarn is straightforward, and you reach the edge of the water at a particularly attractive spot where mature trees fringe and shade the shoreline. These include ash, hazel, lime and oak, and their spreading boughs brush the water. The tranquillity of the scene is completed by groups of bulrushes and other marginal plants prodding up from the depths below.

Continue walking SE around the tarn, keeping near to the edge of the water but avoiding any boggy patches. There are many fine views across the tarn as you proceed, both of the craggy, lower fell-sides from which you have just descended and, as you work your way towards the eastern tip of the water, of the more distant higher fells, including Bow Fell and the Langdale Pikes. The latter

10.1 Loughrigg Tarn and the Langdale Pikes.

*10.2 Sunset over
Loughrigg Tarn.*

views are at their best on clear and sunny, windless days when the surface of the tarn is calm and these high fells are reflected in the still waters. Winter ice or the flowering water-lilies of summer provide the ultimate touch of photogenic perfection. In addition, you are likely to attract a pair of swans, a flock of ducks and scurrying water hens and their chicks, all vying for you to feed them.

Climb up the grassy bank away from the tarn and pass through a wooden gate in the iron railings above. The railings border a driveway along which you turn R. This in turn leads to a gate, after which you turn R up a lane, passing 'Dillygarth Residence'. Then, in quick succession, turn L, R and L again through the maze of lanes and minor roads which converge here, to select the one which leads steeply and most directly down to Skelwith Bridge. The main A593 Ambleside–Coniston road is reached below at MR 345035. Cross over and walk past the Skelwith Bridge Hotel. Immediately

after passing the hotel carpark, turn R and then select the L fork nearest to the River Brathay, to continue along the signed footpath leading W towards Elterwater.

The footpath starts as a surfaced lane which quite conveniently leads to Kirkstone Galleries. These are spacious showrooms, specializing in slate products but also displaying a large selection of traditional gifts and handicraft merchandise; there are also refreshment facilities and toilets. Afterwards, continue W up Great Langdale valley, initially between the quarry worksheds, to reach the path just beyond. This way leads beneath trees to Skelwith Force, down below to your L. These impressive falls are well worth an inspection, but do exercise care, especially if there are children with you. (For further details, see Walk 9.)

Follow the continuation path further W along the valley to reach more open countryside, in the form of low-lying meadows flanking the meandering River Brathay. These are entered through a K-gate, where you are requested to keep to the footpath in crossing this agricultural land. Head towards the small knoll and group of trees straight ahead, walking in line with the distant silhouette of the Langdale Pikes. Then bear to the R of the clump of trees and a small outcrop of exposed rock. Just past this feature, you will need to be vigilant to locate a wooden P-stile on your R, which is positioned near a shallow watercourse in ground that is often wet and boggy. After this you cross a wooden bridge over the stream, and from here a narrow but clear path leads up the slope ahead to reach the B5343 road above. This connection is made directly opposite Silverthwaite carpark.

The road is accessed through a wide gap in the bordering stone wall at a point where the road bends sharply, thus restricting vision in both directions. You should therefore be extremely careful of fast-approaching traffic and, as the entrance to this potential danger spot appears abruptly, keep ahead of children in your final approach from the stream below to make sure the road is clear.

PLACES AND ACTIVITIES OF INTEREST

LOUGHRIGG TARN
This small, sheltered haven of water is situated just below Loughrigg Fell. Circular in shape, it is outstandingly beautiful, with particularly fine views across its reeded waters towards the Langdale Pikes. These are often reflected in superb detail on its glass-like surface. The tarn occupies a shallow basin, no more than about 12m (40ft) deep, but unfortunately there have been fatalities in these benign-looking waters. You should therefore resist the temptation of swimming here, for there are much safer spots elsewhere. Likewise, do not be tempted to slide about on the surface when the tarn is frozen over.

SKELWITH FORCE
See Walk 9.

THE KIRKSTONE GALLERIES
The Galleries are open seven days a week. For further details, contact Kirkstone Galleries (see Useful Addresses, contact telephone numbers).

Kirkstone slate, a natural sea-green stone of volcanic origin which is unique to the Lake District, has been quarried here since Roman times. On show and sale at the galleries are the many items into which Kirkstone can be cut and shaped, including decorative paving, fireplaces, tables, clocks, table mats and even earrings. There is also an excellent coffee shop.

AROUND
GRASMERE AND
AMBLESIDE

11 GRASMERE, RYDAL WATER AND WORDSWORTH

**STARTING/
FINISHING POINT**
Broadgate Meadow
carpark, Grasmere
OLM 7: MR 338077

**GRADING OF
WALK**
Easy/
straightforward

TIME ALLOWANCE
3 hours

DISTANCE
9.9 km (6.1 miles)

**TOTAL HEIGHT
GAINED**
60m (195ft)

HIGHEST POINT
Loughrigg Terrace
120m (395ft)

GRADIENTS
A few gentle to moderate ups and downs

PARKING
The large, well-appointed carpark holds about 80 cars

PUBLIC TRANSPORT
CMS bus routes W1 Bowness pier to Grasmere (Lakeland Experience: open-top service) and 555 Lancaster to Carlisle

GENERAL
The paths are good to excellent, although there is some erosion in places

TACKLING THE WALK

CASUAL WALKERS
This is an almost perfect route for the vast majority of less energetic walkers. It is relatively undemanding, and with good, clear paths for most of the way, superb scenery throughout, an interesting cave to examine and several sites connected with Wordsworth to visit, it is probably a walk you will be happy to retrace time and time again.

FAMILY WALKERS
This route is also eminently suitable for most family groups. Those with younger children may venture no further than the inviting shingle beaches towards the SE tip of Grasmere, for on hot days the safe, gradually sloping ground provides lido-type amenities for picnicking on the grassy slopes and paddling in the shallows below.

Previous page:
Early-morning
tranquillity at
Alcock Tarn.

DEDICATED FELL WALKERS
This is a fine, interesting short route, and with its superb landscapes, caves and Wordsworth connections it should appeal to all

88

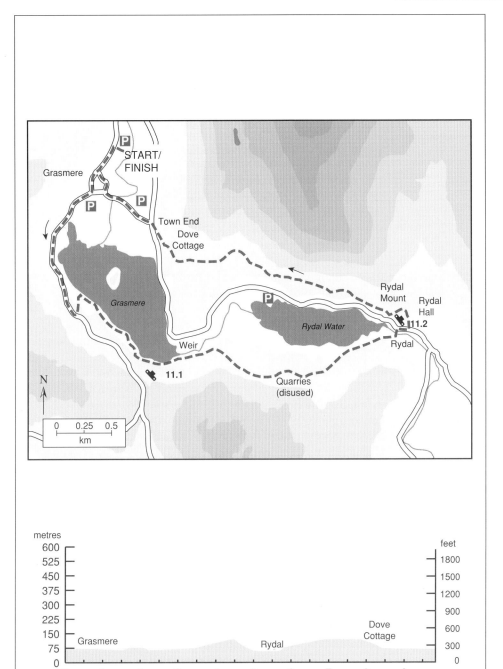

categories of walkers. Alternatively, the route could conveniently be extended to take in the summit of Silver How and perhaps also Loughrigg Fell.

L EAVE Grasmere along the narrow lane running by the side of the Red Lion Hotel, walking SW. Turn R when you reach Red Bank Road carpark to continue along the minor lane which winds around the W of Grasmere (lake) over to Elterwater in Great Langdale. The Information Centre is just across the road to the L. The route continues away from this to the W in the direction of Silver How. Follow the bends of the road as it passes the attractive inlet where rowing boats may be hired and inviting tea gardens are situated. Along here and over to your R as you pass the Gold Rill Hotel there is a clear sighting of Helm Crag over to the NNW. Further round to your R are the higher, rounded fellsides stretching to the summits of Helvellyn and Fairfield.

The road starts to wind uphill as you pass some lovely seclud-ed gardens. These contain massed arrays of rhododendrons and azaleas at their flowering best in May, together with acers, and pro-viding warm, russet leaf tones in autumn. Then, over the dry stone wall on your L, appear the first glimpses of the lake with its tiny, wooded island prominent. Far beyond these sheltered waters, the pinnacle on the horizon is the summit of Wansfell Pike, which overlooks Ambleside to the SE. The gradient steepens as the lane continues to wind uphill between overhanging trees, which include beech, cherry, holly, laurel, oak and sycamore. Ignore a side lane leading off to your R and signed 'Public Footpath to Great Langdale'. However, within 200 paces of passing this you will need to be vigilant to spot a narrow G-stile in the stone walling on the L side of the road. This is positioned just prior to reaching a gate and is at MR 335064. Pass through the stile and follow the obvious foot-path leading down to the lake beneath beech trees.

With superb views appearing across the lake, turn R to begin a delightful stretch of the walk around the western shores of Grasmere. This section close to the water's edge will pass all too quickly as the route threads under copper beech trees and through gates, one of which is a particularly tight squeeze! Turning your gaze from the lake, Loughrigg Fell rises ahead to the SE beyond the far tip of Grasmere, and this first comes into clear view after you have rounded an aged boat house with moss-covered roof slates.

Keep to the edge of the lake until you reach its SE tip, where you pass through a K-gate positioned at the edge of a wooden fence. Then, just before reaching the weir and the footbridge across the River Rothay, bear off R up the fellside along a broad path of compacted earth which leads E. Before proceeding further, turn around to observe the superb view across the lake of the pointed peak of Silver How rising majestically to the WNW. The now stony path begins to rise gently snaking around the bracken-covered fellside above the river. The way continues to the R of a dry stone wall and over the next brow part of Rydal Water appears below to the L, nestling at the bottom of the rounded, folded fellsides which cup the lake. Ignore the railed path leading down to your L and instead bear R along the clearly defined higher path, which tracks at a more or less constant height around the expansive fellsides above Rydal Water. An inviting wooden seat, dedicated to Joe Turner, National Park voluntary warden, is situated along here. Just past it, select the higher path when the way forks. This then rises to connect with Loughrigg Terrace, along which you bear L.

The fairly level, wide stony path leads to and past disused quarry workings complete with spoils and excavated caves. The largest and most impressive of these has recently been closed due to its unstable roof, but when it is made safe again do enter, for the view from the rear of the cave masked by its irregular, black, serrated roof section is quite spectacular. From the entrance to this cave, descend beneath the larch trees towards Rydal Water along the wide, gravel path that winds around the slate spoils. Some less spectacular caves are then passed as the path contorts down the wooded fellside.

Drop down to the edge of Rydal Water and pass through an iron K-gate in a stone wall, having ignored the higher-level alternative route through a gate above. The continuation way is now through Rydal Woods access area. This sheltered, shaded path will lead you to another iron K-gate at the far boundary wall of the woods, and a short distance beyond this the River Brathay is crossed by means of a secure footbridge, accessed through a gate/stile combination. This connects the path with the main A591 Ambleside–Keswick road at MR 364062.

Turn R and cross the busy road, well away from the bends, then turn L up the next lane which leads to the Church of St Mary, Rydal Hall and Rydal Mount. Continue uphill past all three unless you wish to visit these attractions. The church needs no promotion, there are refreshment facilities at the Hall, and you could spend an entire half-day looking around Wordsworth's former home and lux-uriant, semi-formal gardens – and still want to come back for more! The fern-leaved beech tree, *Fagus heterophylla cristata*, is one of the many highlights, as is 'Dora's Field'. Just past the carpark for Rydal Mount, turn L along the public bridleway signed to Grasmere. Then bear L again to avoid walking up the entrance drive to Hart Head Barn, instead passing through the gate to continue along the elevated bridleway.

The way leads through a second gate and then around the more open fellsides as views of Rydal Water appear again, now down to your L. Look ahead beyond these waters to locate the tips of the Langdale Pikes just appearing above the foliage. Keep to the obvious wide, stony path as it tracks WNW, undulating around the tree-covered fellsides. Further on, there are sightings in clear weather of Pike of Blisco, Crinkle Crags and Bow Fell, silhouetted against the skyline to the W. A succession of gates now has to be negotiated, and in among these is an unusual stone seat which occupies a good vantage point.

The way then threads under trees through a more enclosed section, leading beside a dry stone wall on your L. After another gate you come across several choices of way, but any of these will do as they consolidate again a short distance further on. The main criterion is to keep intermittent contact with the dry stone wall on your L and avoid branching off along any of the side paths on your R leading up the steeper fellside. Further on, the tip of Wetherlam and its associated peaks may be observed to the WSW over the wall on your L. Just beyond another gate, avoid the turning to your L and the path leading sharply downhill by continuing straight ahead

11.1 Looking northwards across Grasmere.

93

*11.2
Wordsworth's
home at Rydal
Mount.*

along the enclosed walled way, to pass by the residence named Breckstone.

After crossing a beck, ignore the footpath on your R winding up the open fellside, as this leads to the higher ground housing Alcock Tarn. The path is now surfaced and you pass an interesting, elongated bog pool to your R. These trapped waters are liberally covered with marestail, which attracts both inquisitive ducks and, in summer, multitudes of very active insects. The lane then leads sharply downhill, bending L past another strategically positioned seat from which there are clear views across Grasmere to Silver How to the W. Avoid a second path leading off uphill from here, also towards Alcock Tarn. Instead, continue down the lane and join the narrow back road linking with the A591 road at White Moss, passing a duck pond on your R.

The lane leads further downhill, passing by Dove Cottage and Wordsworth's Museum. A stop at this much-loved attraction is almost mandatory. On the way down, be careful to ignore yet another path leading off to the R. After your visit to Dove Cottage, continue downhill to cross the busy A591 again and then continue along Stock Lane, the loop B5287 road, back into Grasmere village. Here you can visit Wordsworth's grave, which is located at the rear of St Oswald's cemetery just across the River Rothay, in a most appropriate peaceful setting. Further on, use the riverside path to return to your car.

PLACES AND ACTIVITIES OF INTEREST

GRASMERE VILLAGE
See Walk 12.

RYDAL MOUNT
William Wordsworth's home from 1813 until his death in 1850, this superbly located house contains family portraits, personal possessions and first editions. It is surrounded by four acres of fascinating gardens, landscaped by the industrious poet and described as one of the most interesting small gardens to be discovered anywhere in England. The views from these tranquil surroundings are quite magnificent.

Rydal Mount is open daily from March to the following mid-January, but is closed on Tuesdays during the winter months. For a contact telephone number, see Useful Addresses.

DOVE COTTAGE AND THE WORDSWORTH MUSEUM
Dove Cottage was William Wordsworth's home from 1799 to 1808. He wrote many famous works here, including the completion of *The Prelude* (1805). The daily life of the poet and his family is recorded in his devoted sister Dorothy's journals. Visitors are offered guided tours of the cottage and, weather permitting, the garden 'a little nook of mountain-ground' is open. The award-winning Wordsworth Museum illustrates the poet's life and work with manuscripts, portraits and memorabilia.

These attractions are open daily, apart from 24–26 December, the last three weeks in January and the first week in February. For a contact telephone number, see Useful Addresses.

ST OSWALD'S CHURCH AND WORDSWORTH'S GRAVE
St Oswald's Church is located in the centre of Grasmere Village beside the River Rothay. From a distance it is not an awe-inspiring building and has been described by Baddely as 'one of the humblest specimens of ecclesiastical architecture ever in Westmorland'. However, its graveyard does contain the remains of William, Mary and Dorothy Wordsworth, together with Hartley Coleridge, Dora and the two infants who died in Grasmere, and for this reason alone it has become something of a Mecca for those interested in the life and death of the great poet. One other interesting feature of the church is that it serves three parishes and has a separate entrance for each.

12 SILVER HOW AND ROWING BOATS

**STARTING/
FINISHING POINT**
Broadgate Meadow
carpark, Grasmere
OLM 7: MR 338077

**GRADING OF
WALK**
Moderate/
challenging

TIME ALLOWANCE
3 hours

DISTANCE
5.8 km (3.6 miles)

**TOTAL HEIGHT
GAINED**
305m (1000ft)

HIGHEST POINT
Silver How
394m (1295ft)

GRADIENTS

There is a reasonably demanding, steady climb to the top of Silver How, which includes some steep sections

PARKING

The large, well-appointed carpark holds about 80 cars

PUBLIC TRANSPORT

CMS bus routes W1 Bowness pier to Grasmere (Lakeland Experience: open-top service) and 555 Lancaster to Carlisle

GENERAL

The paths are generally quite good, although rough and wet in places. There is some elementary scrambling and occasionally quite severe erosion, but no really serious problems

TACKLING THE WALK

CASUAL WALKERS

This delightful walk, although involving a serious climb, should be well within the capabilities of any reasonably fit walker. The rewards in terms of views and sense of achievement in completing the entire walk will be well worth the effort, and those who do may be spurred into attempting even more strenuous routes in the future. If you attempt the climb and it proves not to your liking, simply retrace your steps back to Grasmere.

FAMILY WALKERS

This route is almost certainly beyond the reasonable capabilities of younger children, although such family groups can be seen on the top of Silver How in good weather and throughout the year. Stronger, older children, perhaps from about 12 years upwards, ought to relish and enjoy the climb, but the sensible advice is not to push this. Obviously, there is no harm in trying the route in favourable weather conditions and, if it proves too much, returning to Grasmere from any point of the climb.

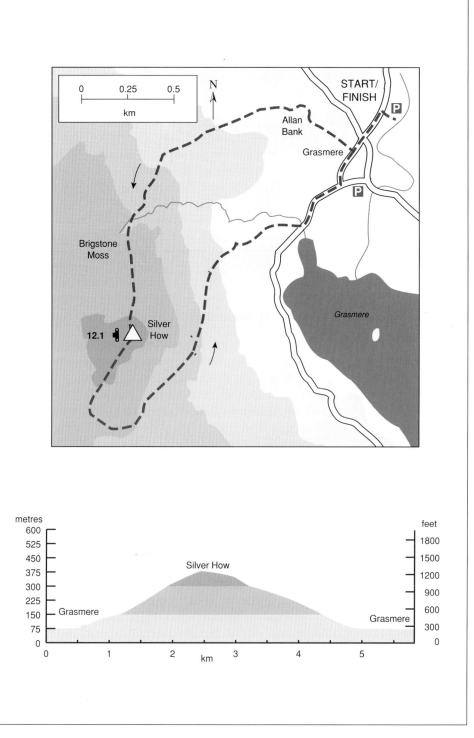

DEDICATED FELL WALKERS

The pull up to the top of Silver How and the superb views both on the way up and from the summit area should appeal to even the strongest of walkers. This climb may be completed at the start of any longer, more arduous route leading w towards Blea Rigg and the higher fells beyond. Alternatively, the complete walk could be used as a delightful way of toning up the muscles at the start of a holiday spent in Lakeland, as a prelude to tackling more demanding, higher walking routes in the days ahead.

FROM the village centre near the Red Lion Hotel, leave along the lane by the side of 'The Coffee Bean', signed 'No Through Road– Public Footpath Score Crag and Silver How'. Your departure direction is to the WNW. You pass Craig Howe and then the lane narrows as it leads gently uphill. Your main objective, the summit of Silver How, now obligingly appears high above to your L, in the WSW. Beyond a cattle grid, the path leads beneath an avenue of lime and sycamore trees through which there are intermittent glimpses of the craggy peak of Helm Crag (The Lion and the Lamb) over to your R. Bear R ahead as directed by the 'Path' sign; from here the way circles through attractive parkland as more open views of the surrounding high fells appear. These include the W flanks of the Fairfield Horseshoe and the rocks of Stone Arthur, high above to the NE. The picturesque buildings of Grasmere also appear, spread out beneath these formidable, protective slopes.

Around the next bend further panoramas come into view, disclosing the rugged terrain and craggy fells surrounding and separating the remote valleys of Easedale and Far Easedale to the NW. The surfaced track winds gradually further uphill by the side of the enclosed deciduous woodlands of Allan Bank on your L. Then, just before reaching two delightfully situated cottages, bear L up the track signed 'Silver How and Langdale' to pass almost immediately through a K-gate. From here a rougher path of stones and boulders winds further uphill, with continuing fine views appearing to your R. The path funnels into a more enclosed section, continuing to snake upwards between a stone wall and a wire fence.

The path changes to a more open, grassy track and this leads to another K-gate providing access to the open fellside. From here, a distinct path winds up the steep slopes ahead towards the juniper-fringed skyline to the SW. The next section is relatively hard going and you should therefore take your time. During wet weather there are invariably soft and boggy areas on these slippery slopes, the worst of which will necessitate some minor detours. During this ascent there is intermittent contact with another dry stone wall to your immediate L.

The immediate rewards for your efforts are the new views as you gain additional height. Grasmere and Loughrigg Fell appear on your L to the SSE and, higher still, the distinctive peak of Wansfell Pike may be observed in clear weather, away to the SE beyond Grasmere (lake). Grasmere (village), spreadeagled below, and its surrounding massive fells complete this magnificent panorama. Eventually the steeper section is conquered, signalled by reaching a cairn positioned at the fringe of the juniper bushes. From here, a narrower path leads off to the L, gaining further height by the side of a confined gully through which a tiny beck trickles. The path tracks on up the fellside, passing further guiding cairns. It then swings abruptly to the R just before another miniature ravine is reached, this one on the L.

A few paces further on, take care to turn L along the less distinctive branch path to cross the enclosed, craggy gully. This is down a rocky chute on your L at MR 326075½. Scramble up the rocky bank opposite and then veer R to locate and follow a faint grassy track which leads southwards across the rounded fellside above. There is another cairn which will confirm your position here. Fortunately, the path soon becomes better established as a line of cairns mark the way. The peak of Silver How appears again around the next bend, now comfortingly much nearer and not so high above! Continue to follow the clearly visible approach route to this peak, walking along a pleasant grassy track towards it. This circles around the intervening fellside to deposit you at the base of the final steeper, eroded approach slopes leading to the summit.

While taking a few deep breaths before scaling to the top, look about you to observe the broad, undulating ridge leading off to your R. This connects with Blea Rigg to the NW and then with the higher ground of Sergeant Man and the Langdale Pikes, further W still. In clear weather the tips of these mighty fells and the pointed peak of Bow Fell may be seen from here. Turning your attention to the task ahead, cross an often boggy area occupying a shallow gully and then climb the final steeper slopes at a steady pace. This section is up a rough, stony path that twists and turns to the top.

The flattish ground around the summit provides the ultimate all-round, secure viewing platform. Many of the fells to be observed from here have been previously seen, but in fine weather there are new and exciting vistas. These include, to the W, Pike of Blisco and Crinkle Crags, the latter connected to Bow Fell by the high hause which contains The Three Tarns, and to the SW the extensive and discrete Coniston Fells rise, with Wetherlam dominating the perspective from here. Windermere snakes away to the SSE, and if you venture a few paces towards the eastern rim of the summit area you will be rewarded with a superb bird's-eye view down over Grasmere and Rydal Water. On the far horizon to the ENE is the

12.1 The westward panorama from near the summit of Silver How.

mighty bulk of Red Screes, and beyond this the tips of the highest parts of the far easterly fells, dominated by High Street. Another fell worth spotting from here is part of Blencathra (Saddleback), some of its arêtes visible through the V-shaped nick between Steel Fell and the Helvellyn range to the N.

Afterwards, be careful to locate the correct way down by following the faint grassy path leading SSW. This is towards a large cairn which is positioned below, just to the R of an alignment with the quarry scar on the far-distant fellside across Great Langdale. There is more than a single track along here, and providing you keep to the higher ground along the descending band in close proximity to the sharply falling ground on your L, which is out of bounds, it matters little which particular track you choose to follow, as they merge further down. However, if there are children with you keep them safely away from the potentially dangerous ground to the L.

Your narrow descent path alternates between a clearly defined, obvious way and more uncertain sections, but fortunately the correct descent line, predominantly to the SSW, is marked by the occasional reassuring cairn. When you reach a much larger cairn, the route tracks down more steeply ahead to the L, along a narrow but distinct path. A relatively steeper and rougher section follows down a craggy, eroded gully, where the path of sorts twists and contorts to reach the lower ground below. There are loose stones and unstable debris in places during this exacting descent, so exercise appropriate care and use your hands to steady your safe progress down where necessary. Fortunately, this section is not lengthy and the worst is soon above you.

The way then straightens out and levels off, leading to an intersection of paths immediately below. Turn L through 90° at this junction, to continue along the wide grassy path which leads E in the direction of Grasmere and Rydal Water. The way then bends around towards the NE, more directly towards Grasmere village. A lengthy, circuitous and more gradual descent follows, which will bring you to a dry stone wall below. Two craggy gullies have to be crossed to get there. Continue down beside the wall, passing the steep, scree-covered, easterly slopes of Silver How on your L in the process. Lower down you will be lucky not to encounter the occasional boggy and waterlogged area crossing a boulder-strewn section of the way.

The obvious descent leads to an important K-gate. This is positioned to your R, where it breaches a stone wall marking the boundary line of open countryside. Squeeze through the gate to enter more sheltered, agricultural lands where you are requested to keep to the designated footpaths. These are of compacted gravel and lead down gentle, wooded slopes towards Grasmere, now to the NE. Other gates follow and the path alternates between a gentle, easy descent and rougher, eroded, more demanding sections. Finally, an enclosed path leads down to the minor road over Red Bank which links Grasmere with Great Langdale.

This road is reached at the entrance to the imposing residence named Kelbarrow, opposite the rowing-boat hire facilities at the N tip of Grasmere (lake). There is a delightful stretch of sheltered, grassy ground here where refreshments may be purchased and consumed in an idyllic setting. After this, follow the road the short distance back into the centre of the village.

PLACES AND ACTIVITIES OF INTEREST

GRASMERE

This charming village, with its strong Wordsworth connections including the poet's former home at Dove Cottage and his grave at St Oswald's church, is situated virtually at the centre of the Lake District and, apart from being the starting point for this splendid walk up Silver How, it offers a range of attractions for the discerning visitor. These include its close proximity to the lake, the River Rothay running through it, its numerous good hotels, boarding houses, cafes and traditional inns, and its tourist shops and picture galleries. In particular, it contains the famous Heaton Cooper and Grieg Hall studios, Sarah Nelson's original, celebrated gingerbread, Sam Read's long-established and well-stocked bookshop and Outdoor World, one of the premier outdoor clothing and equipment retailers in the Lake District. It also has a fine garden centre and a large recreational area. Grasmere is well served by carparks, but these fill up quickly so the advice is to get there early.

SILVER HOW

This prominent fell rises to a height of 394m (1295ft) to the SW of Grasmere. It overlooks the village and lake, and its distinctive summit is part of the Grasmere scene. It also presents a popular climb from the village, as there are magnificent views of the surrounding fells both on the way up and from its lofty top.

BOATING ON GRASMERE

Rowing boats may be hired on Grasmere during the summer months and at other popular times of the year. The boat hire is located on a narrow inlet at the top N end of the lake. This is a really delightful spot, where light refreshments may be purchased and consumed on a shaded, grassy slope which falls gently to the water's edge.

13 ALCOCK TARN AND WORDSWORTH

STARTING/ FINISHING POINT
Broadgate Meadow carpark, Grasmere
OLM 7: MR 338077

GRADING OF WALK
Moderate/ challenging

TIME ALLOWANCE
3 hours

DISTANCE WALKED
4.5km (2.8 miles)

TOTAL HEIGHT GAINED
340m (1115ft)

HIGHEST POINT
Alcock Tarn
375m (1230ft)

GRADIENTS

There is a short, sharp and, in places, steep climb to reach Alcock Tarn

PARKING

The large, well-appointed carpark holds about 80 cars

PUBLIC TRANSPORT

CMS bus routes W1 Bowness pier to Grasmere (Lakeland Experience: open-top service) and 555 Lancaster to Carlisle

GENERAL

The paths vary from very good to rough and demanding, with some erosion. There are some waterlogged areas on the final approach to the tarn

TACKLING THE WALK

CASUAL WALKERS

This walk is suitable for most people who like to be among the Lakeland fells. It offers a steep, challenging start which is not too long, rewarded by superb views, a hidden tarn of great character, an exhilarating descent and an opportunity to visit locations connected with Wordsworth.

FAMILY WALKERS

This route is also suitable for family groups with children above the age of about eight years. To the attractions for casual walkers, add opportunities for fishing.

DEDICATED FELL WALKERS

The steep climb up to Alcock Tarn should appeal to most energetic fell walkers. However, unless it is a before-breakfast or late-evening exercise, it will probably not last long enough. If this is the case, just continue up the steep fellside to Heron Pike, or make a circuit of the whole of the Fairfield Horseshoe while you are there.

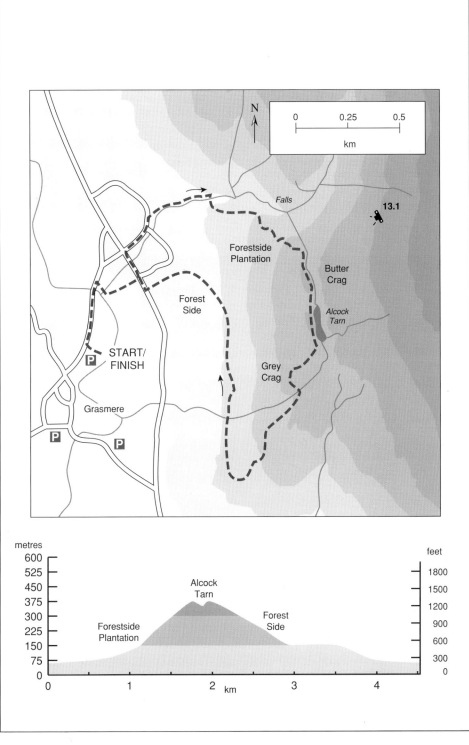

STARTING from the entrance to the carpark, cross over the road, turn R and walk away from the centre of Grasmere along Broadgate. The massive, grassy slopes rising directly ahead lead to the summits of Helvellyn and Fairfield while above, more to your R and nestling out of view just behind the craggy horizon, is Alcock Tarn, your main objective. This is due E. Cross the road again to make maximum use of the pavement, which alternates to either side of the road, and cross over the River Rothay. Turn back R at the next entrance drive to walk past Riversdale and Rothay Lodge guest houses. After this, continue along the way signed 'Pedestrians Only'. An enclosed footpath then leads directly to the A591 road ahead.

Turn L along the road and cross this at a convenient place before reaching the Swan Inn, a short distance further on. To your L the craggy peak of Helm Crag – nicknamed The Lion and The Lamb on account of a rocky upthrust which resembles these animals in profile – soars up to the NW. To your rear and L, the pointed summit of Silver How may be identified to the WSW. Turn R up the lane leading alongside the Swan Inn, walking up the slope to the NE. The crags straight ahead are named Stone Arthur. Keep to the lane as it curves around to the L, avoiding the branch at the bend to the R. Within roughly 100 paces, turn R along the narrow way signed 'Public Footpath – Greenhead Gill – Alcock Tarn'.

13.1 Looking down on Alcock Tarn.

A pleasant walled lane now leads uphill between spacious dwellings and beside the bubbling waters of a fast-flowing, frothy brook which appears anxious to tumble into the River Rothay below. The way leads to a gaggle of three gates: pass through the centre one and then turn R as indicated by the waysign to cross the beck immediately by a narrow railed footbridge. The continuation way then steepens appreciably up a rougher path, sections of which have recently been renovated. Up you must go, climbing a series of zigzags that traverse across a steep gradient. You eventually reach a welcome seat dedicated to the memory of Tennyson (Tim) Oldfield 1892–1978, author of *Come for a Walk with Me*.

After getting back your breath, use the grassy path to make further progress up the steeply rising fellside. The track then rounds an enclosed group of spruce trees, where you should turn around to absorb the magnificent landscapes stretched out to the W. Down below is the sheltered valley which contains Grasmere, both lake and village, and beyond these green, sheltered lands a succession of craggy fells rises progressively, eventually forming the impressive skyline of the Langdale Pikes and Sergeant Man, visible in clear weather. There is a good view of the summit area of Helm Crag, revealing the rocks which make up the 'Lion and Lamb' configuration. Further to the R, towards the NNW, is the flattish, domed crest of Steel Fell, with the pointed, grassy ridge which leads to its extensive summit area clearly revealed.

Now turn R towards the walled conifer enclosure, abandoning the narrow path leading straight ahead towards Heron Pike. This manoeuvre will lead you to another series of zigzags, up which you will quickly gain further height across a more exposed and rougher fellside which rises steeply above the conifer plantation. During this part of the climb, in clear weather, a magnificent array of high fells come into view to your R. These include the Coniston Fells, of which the summit of Wetherlam rising to the SW is dominant when viewed from this perspective. The massed peaks to the W belong to Crinkle Crags. In contrast, part of Grasmere lake appears below, shimmering in its tranquil, wooded setting.

For now, the craggy rock formations above on your L hide the secluded, shallow basin which is filled by the waters of Alcock Tarn. Just press on towards this jagged skyline and all will be revealed! There are several alternative ways of scaling the intervening height, and any will lead you to the flatter ground above. Eventually the steep gradient relents, and when less steep slopes are reached be careful to track around to the R, picking your way between rock outcrops to follow a faint, narrow track.

The continuation way then winds up a gentle grassy slope, passing an unnecessarily large, obtrusive cairn; beyond this, skirt to the R to avoid the worst of a boggy area which appears here to be a permanent feature. The path leads to a stile positioned near a gate in a stone wall. Alcock Tarn, which lies just ahead, is revealed from this gateway. Walk the full length of the narrow, reeded tarn, heading southwards. There is a dam at the southern tip which has raised the water level. The tarn is a tranquil oasis, a quiet place among the most magnificent scenery.

From the far end, leave the tarn on a diagonal to your R, heading SW in line with the far-away Coniston Fells. The grassy track leads to a gap in the dry stone wall directly ahead. Having passed through this, part of distant Windermere may be observed below to your L. A clearly defined, well-used path winds down the fellside, leading back towards Grasmere, at present far below. The worn track contorts down the steep fellside and there are some sharp twists and turns to look out for, as not all are obvious.

Lower down the going becomes progressively less demanding as long, diagonal traverses descend through the gentler bracken-covered slopes. The way then leads past a group of feathery larch trees and a gateway is reached as the path curves lower down the fellside, passing by an area of foxgloves. Keep to the broad, winding path down, avoiding a way leading off to your L through an iron gate. After passing a bench, the way leads past a tiny pool to a division of paths below. Your route is to the R, heading N and dropping downhill. Proceed through the K-gate ahead to continue downwards along a pleasant grassy path.

Keep to the R ahead, choosing the higher, more distinct of two ways forward. This leads to a stream, which you cross by means of a rather unusual footbridge containing an iron frame. The route then traverses around the fellside for some distance at a fairly constant height, until you reach a wooden stile. After this, be careful to turn sharply L downhill in the direction indicated by a sign. This turn is made just before you reach a wooden seat in a grassy clearing. A narrow permitted path then carries on further downhill, making its way through dense bracken. Further on a wider, signed footpath leads beside a boundary wall to a L-stile over a stone wall.

Continue past the bench and another grassy section of the permitted path will lead you first beside a wire fence and then a wall, down to a waymarked gate on your L. Just below this entrance is the carparking area of the superbly located Forest Side Countywide guest house, which caters specially for the walking fraternity. Walk directly across this parking area and then down the entrance drive to reach the main road below. Cross the road on a diagonal to your R, ignoring the public footpath immediately opposite. Turn R along the road and after about 50 paces branch off L to return to Grasmere along the footpath you used towards the start of the walk. From here, retrace your outward steps back to the carpark.

ALTERNATIVE DESCENT PASSING DOVE COTTAGE

There is a convenient alternative descent for those who wish to visit Dove Cottage on foot. When you reach the division of ways just below the tiny pool at MR 344½073, instead of turning R, bear L and follow the obvious path through the woodland southwards to reach the lanes which converge at How Top. Turn R here and walk downhill to reach Dove Cottage, below on the R. After visiting the cottage, continue down the lane, cross over the main A591 road with care and use the loop B5287 to reach the centre of Grasmere, where Wordsworth's last resting place in the cemetery of St Oswald's church may also be visited *en route* back to the car park.

PLACES AND ACTIVITIES OF INTEREST

GRASMERE
See Walk 12.

ALCOCK TARN
The enlarged waters of this tarn command a maximum depth of only about 2m (6ft). The former, natural catchment was known as Butter Crag Tarn, a name derived from the rocky outcrop just to the N. Several plants thrive in the tarn during the summer months including pondweed, water horsetail and reeds. Brown trout were introduced in the nineteenth century, and smaller fry and tadpoles in season will keep visiting youngsters occupied.

DOVE COTTAGE, THE WORDSWORTH MUSEUM,
ST OSWALD'S CHURCH AND WORDSWORTH'S GRAVE
See Walk 11.

14 STOCKGHYLL FORCE, WANSFELL PIKE AND JENKIN CRAG

**STARTING/
FINISHING POINT**
Rydal Road carpark,
Ambleside OLM 7:
MR 376047

**GRADING
OF WALK**
Moderate/
Challenging

TIME ALLOWANCE
3½ hours

DISTANCE
6.2km (3.8 miles)

**TOTAL HEIGHT
GAINED**
450m (1475ft)

HIGHEST POINT
Wansfell Pike
484m (1590ft)

GRADIENTS

It is up all the way to the summit of Wansfell Pike. Part of this climb is steep, up fields which do become slippery, with some eroded sections

PARKING

Massive car park, but with premium charges for a long stay

PUBLIC TRANSPORT

CMS bus routes W1 Bowness pier to Grasmere (Lakeland Experience: open-top service), 505/6 Ambleside to Coniston, Hawkshead and Hilltop (The Coniston Rambler), 516 Ambleside to Dungeon Ghyll (The Langdale Rambler), 555 Lancaster to Carlisle

GENERAL

The paths are good and clear for much of the way, but rough and less distinct in several places. There is significant erosion in the approach to the summit, which is being addressed. Route finding is tricky in places

TACKLING THE WALK

CASUAL WALKERS

The route is well within the capabilities of all reasonably fit walkers and the attractions of the walk are the same as for dedicated fell walkers. Just take a bit longer doing the circuit and allow yourselves a few more stops on the way up!

FAMILY WALKERS

The walk is fine for those with older, stronger youngsters who should enjoy the climb to the top of Wansfell Pike immensely. Most small children will enjoy the visit to Stockghyll Force and below the falls, near the village, there are some flat areas with safe access to the beck which might also appeal.

DEDICATED FELL WALKERS

Although relatively short, this route should appeal strongly to more serious walkers. Stockghyll Force attracts both walkers as well as

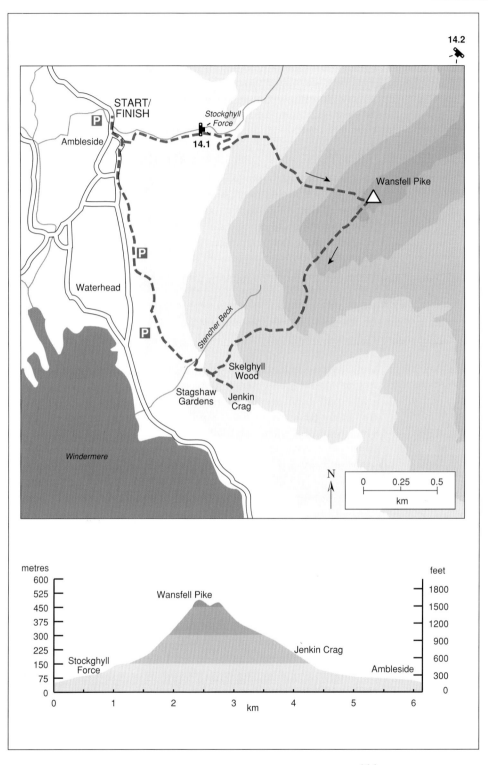

14.2

START/
FINISH

P

Ambleside

*Stockghyll
Force*

14.1

Wansfell Pike

Waterhead

P

P

Stencher Beck

Skelghyll
Wood

Stagshaw
Gardens

Jenkin
Crag

Windermere

N

0	0.25	0.5
km		

metres		feet
600		1800
525	Wansfell Pike	1500
450		
375		1200
300		900
225	Jenkin Crag	
150		600
Stockghyll		
Force	Ambleside	300
75		
0		0

0 1 2 3 4 5 6
km

111

general visitors; there is a steep, demanding climb to the top of Wansfell Pike, superb views when you get there, an interesting descent which calls for some navigational skills, and finally a stroll through deciduous woodlands and a peep from the rocks of Jenkin Crag. The descent from Wansfell Pike may be extended considerably by looping down into Troutbeck and returning to Ambleside along Robin Lane and the bridleways beyond, leading to Jenkin Crag from the SE.

L EAVING the carpark, cross Stock Ghyll and turn R towards the centre of Ambleside. Cross over the road and turn L between the Salutation Hotel and Barclays Bank. Walk past Briggs Shoe Mine and turn L along the lane leading uphill by the side of the wooded valley through which Stock Ghyll tumbles. Just beyond an attractive estate of white-painted houses, turn off L to enter Stock Ghyll Park and continue along the footpaths towards the waterfalls. A pleasantly shaded, waysigned route leads uphill above the R bank of the stream. Sections of this way are stepped, as the route continues to ascend through deciduous woodland of beech, hazel, holly and sycamore.

Just before reaching a wooden bench, fork L to descend a stepped way, before crossing the beck over the wooden footbridge below. Climb up the steep flight of steps on the far side, keeping to the path indicated by the red arrowhead waysigns. Be mindful of the steep fall-away to your R along here, particularly if there are young children with you. You are now climbing some height above what has developed into a steep-sided ravine to your R, with the gurgling waters of Stock Ghyll a frothing ribbon continually eroding its base way below. When you reach another section of steps, branch R along the railed, dead-end side path to obtain a superb view of the higher falls and the attractive footbridge which spans these above. Exercise great care at this exposed viewing position, as there are potential dangers.

Return to the main path and complete your climb to the footbridge spanning the falls. Cross over this and walk back down the southern slopes of the ravine, negotiating a rocky section in the process. Branch L when you reach a fork in the path lower down, disregarding the direction indicated by the arrowhead positioned at this junction. More red waymarkers are located ahead, before the path leads to an unusual metal turnstile gateway which you pass through. Turn L on the far side to walk uphill along the lane, which is also signed as a public footpath. The route passes by the entrance to Force Close, after which the surface deteriorates as it now serves Grove Farm only; cross the protective cattle grid inserted in it.

14.1 Spring at Stockghyll Force.

Continue walking uphill as more open views appear on your L of the fells and valley systems which rise towards the Fairfield Horseshoe. In very clear weather, to your rear and L the distinctive helmets of the Langdale Pikes may be observed to the NW. After passing a bench dedicated to John Huntington, be careful to turn sharp R along the footpath signed to Troutbeck via Wansfell. This is accessed by climbing up an iron ladder and hopping over a P-stile. From here a clear, well-used path tracks up the open grassy fell-sides, keeping company with a beck down on your L. At this point the summit of Wansfell Pike, your main objective, comes into view, rising majestically to the ESE.

The obvious continuation path leads to a L-stile over a high stone wall at the top edge of the field. Safely over this, cross the end of the walled track on the far side, step over the remains of a fallen tree which has remained here for ages and continue the steep climb up the grassy slopes ahead, gaining additional height to the SE. These steep, often slippery fellsides will test your resolve and there will be few walkers who do not puff and pant up these demanding gradients, so take your time and stop now and again to admire the views and to get your breath back. The landscapes now appearing below are quite magnificent. The best of these are to the W beyond the sprawling village of Ambleside, where the Langdale valleys quite naturally lead your eyes towards the huge cradle of high peaks which include Wetherlam, Crinkle Crags, Bow Fell and the Langdale Pikes.

Further up still an erosion control area is reached, and you are requested to keep to the refurbished sections of path which are being extended progressively. Cross a tiny watercourse on your L by a wooden footbridge, after which the more secure, refurbished way leads further up the knobbly, grassy fellside. From this vantage point, in clear weather, most of the extensive Fairfield Horseshoe is revealed away to the NNW, while further R the massive ridge culminating in Red Screes may be observed to the NNE. Further R still, some of the far easterly spurs rising to High Street also come into view. The newly constructed tiered path winds up and up as the views of the landscapes below improve still further.

After scaling a final rocky chute on the L or selecting one of the alternative craggy ways to the top and perhaps benefiting from using more recently refurbished sections, you will reach the helmet-shaped outcrop of rock which forms the summit area of Wansfell Pike. The panoramic views from this barren rock are fantastic if you are favoured with clear visibility. Many of the fells in view from here have been sighted already, but the new vistas to the S along the length of Windermere are breathtaking, and the sunsets from here rank among the finest to be observed anywhere in Lakeland.

114

Wander around the extensive summit area, crossing the tall L-stile to stand on the very highest point of the fell and observe every perspective. From looking down the length of Windermere, if you slowly rotate clockwise around the compass points you will view, in succession, the Coniston Fells, Crinkle Crags, Bow Fell, the Langdale Pikes, the Fairfield Horseshoe, Red Screes and the easterly fells, of which the pointed peak of Ill Bell is most dominant. Carefully cross the high stile again and begin your descent by scrambling down the rough, rocky path to your L. Climb down to reach the grassy ledge a short distance below to the SW. Here, cross the dry stone wall on your L by means of the huge L-stile, turning around at the top to climb down in safety.

Now bear R along the narrow grassy path, following the line of the wall on your R as you descend across the undulating ground ahead. The route leads SW and this will remain your predominant direction as you lose height progressively, walking towards Windermere. The lake is spreadeagled below among gently rounded, wooded slopes. A steeper, rougher section downhill, adjacent to the wall, leads you to a stile on the R which you climb over to continue down the clearly waysigned route (white arrowheads). From here, the route traverses around the craggy, bracken-covered fellsides, following a newly developed circular route which is becoming increasingly popular with walkers. The correct way down does become somewhat obscure in places, but by looking ahead you should be able to locate the clearer continuation route without too much difficulty.

The way down leads to and passes to the L of a fenced-off area of long-abandoned quarry workings. From here, a grassy path winds L further downhill, to reach a waterlogged crossing of flatter ground below. Veer L beyond this, walking more southwards to pass to the L of a craggy outcrop, passing beneath this along a grassy path. The track then swings back R to reach and pass through a gap in the stone wall directly ahead, at which a redundant gate is left permanently open. Continue downhill to the SSW along a now obvious grassy way and pass through a second open gateway.

Continue straight ahead, still making headway to the SW, and further on use a section of cart track for a short distance. However, before this track leads into forbidden agricultural land (National Trust sign), turn sharp R to resume your descent along a grassy path. The way then becomes less clear again; be careful here to cross another wet area below, before locating the narrow continuation path to the L of a shallow, grassy gully, converging on a dry stone wall ahead. For a short distance your direction tracks somewhat surprisingly NW, in line with the Fairfield Horseshoe. Locate a narrow but clear path which then tracks through bracken above wetter ground.

14.2 Wansfell
Pike viewed
from the
Kirkstone Road.

The path leads down to a stone pillar (there are several more in this area) which is marked on the OLM at MR 386033. A short distance below this feature, the now clearly defined path leads to a recently positioned L-stile over the dry stone boundary walling of Skelghyll Wood. This provides welcome shade on hot, sunny days as you track further downhill, following a delightful route through the trees along a narrow path, which leads to a junction of wider paths below. Turn L here and then veer R at the second intersection a few paces further on, to continue your descent through the deciduous woodland. The obvious way then winds down Kelsick Scar, to reach the wide bridleway below near to the popular observation point of Jenkin Crag. Turn L along the bridleway and within 100 paces turn off to the R to complete the short approach to the rounded rocks of the crag.

Jenkin Crag is a popular viewing spot and refreshment stop, and the views from this elevated vantage point looking down and across the upper reaches of Windermere are superb. Wray Castle and the wooded indents to the N are exposed, and in clear weather it is a joy to locate all the landforms visible from here. However, there is a steep, precipitous fall at the far end of the rocks and you should therefore keep a tight hold of any young children that are with you. When you have rested and seen enough, return to the bridleway and turn L to resume your journey back towards Ambleside. Just keep walking down following the broad, obvious track, and when you reach a choice of descents either will do because they merge again a short distance lower down. After this, be careful to cross Stencher Beck ahead, having avoided a steeper side path leading down on your L just before reaching the curved bridge across this watercourse.

Bear R at the bottom of the slope ahead to continue northwards towards the village, keeping always to the main path, a section of which is fenced lower down. The surface improves, mainly for the benefit of vehicles, and the descending traverse provides a bird's-eye view of Hayes Garden Centre spread out below. Turn R when you reach the lane below and follow this into the centre of Ambleside.

PLACES AND ACTIVITIES OF INTEREST

STOCKGHYLL FORCE
This is a series of spectacular waterfalls, fed by the catchment waters of Stock Ghyll tumbling down the rocky ravine to the E of Ambleside. The chasm is densely wooded and the falls are observed most clearly in the winter months, when views of them from the surrounding pathways are not obscured by dense foliage. Most visitors climb to the top of the spectacular cascades and cross the beck above the falls by the attractive bridge, to descend along the opposite bank of the stream from the one up which they have climbed.

JENKIN CRAG
This is a popular viewing point situated in Skelghyll Wood high above the NE tip of Windermere. It is a favourite perch for walkers and birds alike, and the latter will not hesitate to share your lunch or refreshments with you if you give them half a chance! The spot is a mixture of large, rounded boulders and rocks, with a precipitous fall-away that needs to be treated with care, especially if there are youngsters with you. The gentle, wooded landscapes down across Windermere are outstanding, and in fine weather every nook and cranny of the shoreline of Windermere in the vicinity of Wray Castle is exposed from this strategic position.

PATTERDALE, GLENRIDDING AND ULLSWATER

15 BOAT TRIP ON ULLSWATER AND LAKESIDE WALK FROM HOWTOWN

STARTING/ FINISHING POINT
Boat jetty at Glenridding OLM 5: MR 390169. Walk starts from the boat pier Howtown Wyke (MR 443199) and finishes back at Glenridding pier

GRADING OF WALK
Easy/ straightforward

TIME ALLOWANCE
4 hours

DISTANCE
10.5km (6.5 miles)

TOTAL HEIGHT GAINED
245m (805ft)

HIGHEST POINT
Above Ullswater 210m (690ft)

Previous pages: *Autumn reflections in Ullswater.*

GRADIENTS
Some of the slopes are relatively steep but they are all quite short

PARKING
Large, reasonably priced carpark adjacent to the boat jetty

PUBLIC TRANSPORT
CMS bus routes 108 Penrith to Patterdale (The Patterdale Bus) and 517 Bowness to Glenridding (The Kirkstone Rambler)

GENERAL
The clear paths are quite stony and rough in places but there is virtually no waterlogged or boggy ground

TACKLING THE WALK

CASUAL WALKERS
This is a suitable route for the majority of walkers who enjoy being beside water when exploring the craggy fells. It is not too demanding, and although there are some ups and down along a relatively rough path the rewards more than compensate for the effort involved.

FAMILY WALKERS
The boat trip and walk back along Ullswater is a firm favourite with many families, even those with younger children. It usually takes up most of an enjoyable day, including beach-combing distractions. Try it, and before you reach the point of 'no return', if you think it is going to be too much or the children are not really enjoying the outing, settle for a rest and play by the lake, before retracing your steps back to Howtown.

DEDICATED FELL WALKERS
This is an excursion worth undertaking when you feel like a day away from strenuous walking among the high fells. It could also

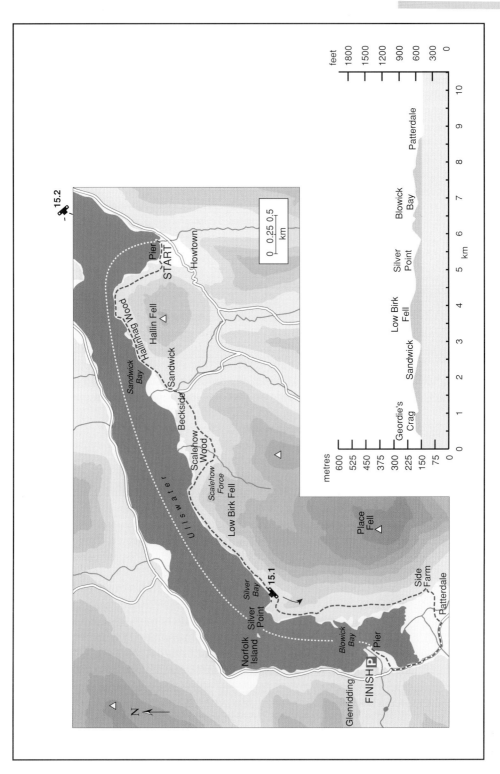

15.2

START
Pier
Howtown

Sandwick Wood
Hallinhag Wood
Hallin Fell △
Sandwick
Sandwick Bay
Beckside

Scalehow Wood
Scalehow Force
Low Birk Fell

U l l s w a t e r

15.1
Silver Bay

Norfolk Island
Silver Point

Blowick Bay
Pier

△

N
△

Glenridding
FINISH P

Side Farm
Patterdale

Place Fell △

0 0.25 0.5
km

metres
600
525
450
375
300
225
150
75

feet
1800
1500
1200
900
600
300
0

Geordie's Crag Sandwick Low Birk Fell Silver Point Blowick Bay Patterdale
0   1   2   3   4   5 km 6   7   8   9   10

be used as a most appropriate walk to show off the wonderful scenery of Lakeland to your less energetic companions. Alternatively, Place Fell could be scaled or you could walk back via Boredale if you prefer a little more exercise. Place Fell is a much-neglected mountain: in clear weather, the views towards Helvellyn and down the length of Ullswater from its extensive summit are fantastic, and if you have not stood on this Place before you are in for a real treat.

THE boat trip with which this outing begins takes just over half an hour and you should plan to catch the earliest possible sailing from Glenridding pier. Given fine weather, this short journey north-eastwards around Place Fell to the sheltered moorings of Howtown Wyke will give you time to absorb the magnificent mountain scenery cupping the southern end of Ullswater. As the launch glides down the lake the craggy slopes of Place Fell rise steeply to your R, effectively blocking off any more distant views in that direction. The lakeside path, snaking along in places just above the waterline and at other points rising abruptly to mount rocky spurs which protrude into the lake, is your return route. There are more open landscapes on the other side of the narrow lake. Beyond the lower crags bordering Ullswater, vast valleys and intervening rocky spurs sweep upwards towards the towering summits of Fairfield, Helvellyn and The Dodds.

After disembarking at Howtown Pier, turn R over the elevated footbridge across Fusedale Beck and follow the obvious footpath which winds W below Hallin Fell. The way then passes beneath a row of sheltering silver birch trees and ahead you may have to queue to pass through the K-gate, which in any event is a tight squeeze.

The picturesque hamlet of Howtown appears over to your L, with its attractive huddle of buildings located beneath steep, conifer-covered fellsides. Through a second K-gate, veer R along a gravel-surfaced lane, but within 60 paces turn off L and pass through another K-gate to reach the footpath signed 'Patterdale and Sandwick'. The track leads through a fenced section and then slightly uphill beside a dry stone wall, winding away from the lake. Climb some steps to reach another gate and, after passing through, turn immediately R to follow the rough, stony path which circles around Hallin Fell, gaining further height in the process.

Within a short distance the upward gradient levels off, and from here there are fine views to your R across and along Ullswater. These disclose the rounded bay where the pier at Howtown Wyke is located. The way then continues at a fairly constant height beside a dry stone wall; after heavy rain there will be some muddy patches

along here. Vast grassy slopes now rise steeply on your L, sweeping up towards the craggy outcrops forming the skyline above. The obvious path then starts to descend, and this marks the first of several undulations along the route. When you reach a spreading oak tree bear L, following the elevated way and parting company with the dry stone wall. You will pass a seat as the route threads across bracken-laden slopes before rounding the rocky headland of Geordie's Crag, after which the route descends gently towards Hallinghag Wood. This woodland is a designated Site of Special Scientific Interest (SSSI) and should be respected as such.

15.1 Ullswater and Place Fell.

Enter the trees at another K-gate, positioned above a particularly attractive stretch of shoreline. This consists of a grassy bank descending towards a rocky promontory and a sheltered shingle beach. The deciduous woods contain a pleasing mixture of beech and oak, and those trees nearest the water's edge provide welcome shade should you wish to stop for refreshments at one of the secluded picnic spots in the sheltered bays which you pass. Meanwhile, the rocky path continues to wind westwards under the trees just above the lake; further on you pass a small wooded knoll on your R. The path then narrows as it rises again to pass over another small, craggy headland. More of the same follows before the route descends to reach Sandwick Bay, where the woodlands terminate.

The final approach to the sheltered bay is to the R along the main path and then through another K-gate. Sandwick Bay is a really delightful spot, with sweeping sands and a tree-fringed backcloth. The footpath then leads away from the lakeside, passing through

123

*15.2 Ullswater
and Glenridding.*

three gates in quick succession along a way signed 'Public Footpath Sandwick'. An elevated path then leads across slopes covered with bluebells in May, through another gate and into Sandwick. The craggy slopes of Place Fell loom up ahead, but in order to walk around these you must next cross Sandwick Beck at MR 424197. This is achieved by turning L and using the sturdy road bridge to cross above the fast-flowing stream, and then passing through a gate on the far side.

From here, follow the surfaced road uphill to your L, avoiding private ground both ahead and to your R. Within a short distance, select the public footpath which leads further up the fell by the side of Townhead Cottage. As you climb up the slope the vast spaces of Boredale and Martindale open up to your L, divided and flanked by parallel craggy spurs which rise to the highest ground of the easterly fells, far away to the S. The route then connects with a better-established cart track ahead, along which you bear R. This wide, stony bridleway rises gently, threading WSW towards the intimidating steep slopes of Place Fell directly ahead.

The clearly defined path now leads past a barn and across a mountain stream. From here on keep to the wide path which winds around the indented shores of Ullswater, studiously avoiding all side paths off to your L, as these rise steeply up the craggy fellside and would eventually take you to the summit of Place Fell. You then cross the cascading waters at the exit of Scalehow Force. These thrash noisily down a narrow, boulder-strewn gully, but your crossing is out of harm's way over a secure, fenced footbridge. Beyond this crossing, the route continues along its now well-established undulating way around or over more rocky headlands and promontories which jut out into the lake below.

Where directed, follow the waysigned (blue arrowhead) alternative paths, which have been established to avoid eroded ground and to give this route an opportunity to recover. The elevated path then passes through strips of silver birch and hawthorn which are spectacular in their autumn finery, the yellows, oranges and browns set against the blues of Ullswater glimpsed through wavering gaps between the fading leaves. There are also more magnificent long-range views across the lake. These include the panorama backwards towards Hallin Fell and also that to the NW towards the densely wooded dell on the far side of Ullswater, which conceals Aira Force (see Walk 16).

The snaking lake, and your route around it, then bends progressively to the L, finally pointing southwards towards Patterdale. As it completes this manoeuvre you will pass along one of the most interesting sections of the entire walk around rocky crags, over rockfalls, and past steep scree- and boulder-ridden slopes where you hope all will remain stable until you have passed by. There are a few strategically positioned side paths off to the R to take you to several beaches and promontories if you have the time and inclination for such a detour. The most severe of the upward gradients do present temporary challenges which might sway you in favour of a cooling breather down by the water's edge. Afterwards, loop back to the main bridleway leading s.

A favourite promontory with many walkers is Silver Point just to the E of tiny Norfolk Island. From and beyond this fine headland more revealing landscapes appear, including those across the lake beyond Glenridding and your starting point at the steamer jetty towards St Sunday Crag, Fairfield and Helvellyn, towering above to the SW. The route then meanders uphill towards a group of conifer trees silhouetted against the skyline. A sign along here confirms that you are still heading towards Patterdale. The obvious continuation path then descends gradually to bring you to Side Farm to the SSE. There are often muddy patches along here, and a stream will have to be forded, while an L-stile over the stone wall on your R and a fork to the L leading up the fell must be avoided. The farm offers light refreshments, as well as horse riding.

Pass through the gate into the farmyard and then turn R to follow the path signed to Patterdale–Glenridding. This is along the farm entrance lane across low-lying pastures, which can become flooded after prolonged heavy rain (in this event, there is a road bridge across Goldrill Beck a short distance further along the valley). The preferred route crosses over two cattle grids positioned on either side of Goldrill Beck, to reach the main A592 road through Patterdale and Glenridding. This connection is at MR 394161 near the George Starkey Hut, Club Alpin Suisse 1863.

Turn R along the road and follow this back into Glenridding, making full use of the pavements and adjacent paths on either side of the busy road wherever possible. You will pass St Patrick's Church at Patterdale in the process. Finally, branch off along the path to the R past Ullswater Boat Stores to return to the steamer jetty and carpark.

PLACES AND ACTIVITIES OF INTEREST

ULLSWATER MOTOR YACHTS
Raven and *Lady of the Lake* are two nineteenth-century steamers, now converted to oil, cruising on Ullswater. Ullswater is about 15km (9 miles) long and the yachts ply regularly between Glenridding and Pooley Bridge, located at either end of the lake, stopping at Howtown *en route*. Both vessels have licensed bars and serve hot drinks. There are also toilets on board.

For a timetable, details of private charters and so on, contact Ullswater Navigation and Transit Co Ltd (see Useful Addresses).

16 AIRA FORCE, DOCKRAY AND COMMON FELL

STARTING/ FINISHING POINT
National Trust carpark serving Aira Force, Ullswater
OLM 5: MR401201

GRADING OF WALK
Moderate/ challenging

TIME ALLOWANCE
3½ hours

DISTANCE
7 km (4.2 miles)

TOTAL HEIGHT GAINED
390m (1280ft)

HIGHEST POINT
Common Fell
553m (1815ft)

GRADIENTS

The route rises progressively from the carpark to the summit of Common Fell, with two well-spaced but more challenging slopes, the first up steps to reach the top of Aira Force, and the second across steep, rough fell-sides to the summit of Common Fell. There is also a steep, rocky descent into the quarry carparking area at MR 396211

PARKING

Large, well-screened carpark with toilets, and a cafe nearby. There is also an area for coaches

PUBLIC TRANSPORT

CMS bus route 108 Penrith to Patterdale (The Patterdale Bus)

GENERAL

At the beginning and end of the walk the paths are clear and good. From Dockray to the summit of Common Fell you cross open ground with only intermittent tracks as a guide, so a compass is essential

TACKLING THE WALK

CASUAL WALKERS

This route is within the capabilities of most reasonably fit walkers. However, it does involve some off-path sections across the open fellside and a demanding descent down a rough, steep section of path. Choose good weather for this exploration, when navigational challenges will be minimized and long-distance views will reward you for your efforts. This taste of wilder, more rugged countryside could well give you a healthy appetite for sterner walks. If you have doubts about tackling the entire route, follow the advice for family walkers below.

FAMILY WALKERS

The walk is probably suitable for most strong, hardy teenagers but again select a day when visibility is good and route-finding easier.

128

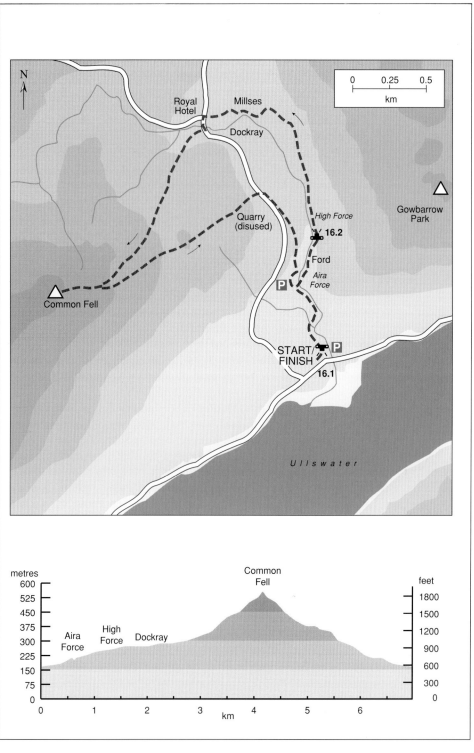

Royal
Hotel

Millses

Dockray

0   0.25   0.5
km

Gowbarrow
Park

High Force

ℵ **16.2**

Quarry
(disused)

Ford

*Aira
Force*

P

Common Fell

START/
FINISH

P

16.1

U l l s w a t e r

N

metres
600
525
450
375
300
225
150
75
0

Common
Fell

feet
1800
1500
1200
900
600
300
0

Aira
Force

High
Force   Dockray

0   1   2   3   4   5   6
km

The complete route is definitely too long and demanding for younger children. These family groups should settle for either a stroll up to the first, spectacular drops of Aira Force or, if they feel they can competently tackle a longer route, walk as far as Dockray and then use the A5091 road for about 0.5km (⅓ mile) to rejoin the main route at MR 397211.

DEDICATED FELL WALKERS

This walk should appeal to most hard men and women of the hills. Although it is relatively short, and for these walkers not very demanding, it will lead many across open fellsides into new ground and provide them with a fresh perspective of some better-known, higher fells.

LEAVE from the top end of the carpark, walking northwards up the valley away from the road. There is usually a National Trust Information Point in the form of a parked Land Rover positioned near the swing exit gate and the knowledgeable personnel manning this vehicle are always very helpful in responding to any queries you may have concerning Aira Force or its surrounds. A wide gravel path leads up the shallow slope ahead threading through an attractive mixture of mature conifers and broadleaved trees. This railed-off way is first class, and when not raining is usually as dry as a bone.

Turn R ahead to pass through a second swing gate, this one positioned in a dry stone wall. The way then passes across a narrow stream at which part of a hollowed-out tree trunk is located. It is almost obligatory for small children to climb through this! Turn almost immediately L along the branch path which winds further up the narrowing, steepening, wooded valley, where a seat is passed on your R. The obvious, well-trodden route then climbs above Aira Beck, visible through the trees below on your R. Sections of steps are climbed next as the narrow path threads its way through encroaching bracken. Keep R when the path divides ahead, and do not pass through the swing gate to the L. Then, just past another seat, turn sharp R to descend down the steep flight of steps to reach the bottom of the main drop of Aira Force.

The waterfalls, tumbling down a narrow, rocky chasm and crashing into a deep, dark catchment pool at their base, are a fantastic sight. Spray billows about everywhere when the beck is in spate, and if you are fortunate these suspended water droplets cause the sunlight to become defracted into multiple rainbow-like spectrums of colour. There are attractive arched bridges spanning the stream above and below the main falls. Use the lower one, just off to your R, to cross Aira Beck. Climb up another stepped path on the far side, taking care to turn sharp L to use the correct continuation flight of railed, slate steps which zigzags more steeply up the fellside. When you reach the higher ground, avoid two paths leading off on your R and instead bear L to make your way to the higher bridge to stand at the mid-point of this arch.

There are more fine views of the falls from this commanding position, well above the spray and turmoil below. Walk the few paces back to regain the main path and turn L along it to resume your progress northwards up the valley beside Aira Beck, up more steps. Climb a short flight of steps on your R to bring you out of the confines of the wooded valley and lead you away from the stream. You will then reach another wooden seat positioned at the boundary of open country. Cross the stile at this boundary and continue along the path ahead. This connects at an acute angle with a wider, better-established track above. Veer L along the combined way to continue northwards above the main belt of trees hugging the meandering watercourse to your L.

Turn around now to observe, in fine weather, a clear view of the St Sunday Crag ridge leading up over Cofa Pike to the broad, flat summit of Fairfield, far away to the SW. The mixture of craggy fell-sides to the R of this ridge leads eventually to Helvellyn and Catstye Cam, both situated to the N of Fairfield. A broad, eroded path then leads further uphill along a gentle, undemanding slope, still follow-ing the course of Aira Beck. Climb over the P-stile ahead and walk past several side paths coming in on your L as you track up the

16.1 Walking towards Aira Force.

widening valley. Some distance further on contact is re-established with the beck. This is at a particularly attractive spot where there are more modestly sized waterfalls, together with smoothed rocks through which water channels flow.

Cross a tributary beck, beyond which the way leads to enclosed farmlands higher up the broadening valley. These lands are entered through a swing gate positioned in a stone wall running at right angles to your approach. From here, the route is uphill again for a short distance under the cooling shade of trees, before you once again penetrate more open ground. Cross another beck and, following this, a straight path leads across gentle, grassy slopes still northwards up the widening valley, which is now quite shallow. In good weather the view to your rear now reveals a long section of Ullswater, snaking away below the massive bulk of Place Fell which rears up to the s of the lake. Nearer to you, the extensive slopes of Gowbarrow rise more uniformly on your immediate L when facing down the valley.

Beyond the next swing gate there is a rare treat in that the route drops down for the first time in winding to your L to cross a trickle of a stream. Avoid the path off to Ulcat Row on your R and continue along the wide, grassy cart track down towards Dockray. A wooden beam spans the next watercourse, named Riddings Beck, after which the track winds around the attractive cottage located at Millses. From here, the path leads slightly uphill again to reach the tiny hamlet of Dockray, passing through another wooden gate before veering R at the junction of tracks ahead. Cross over the road to reach the Royal Hotel, where you may wish to purchase refreshments at very reasonable prices.

From the hotel, turn s along the A5091 road, walking towards Ullswater and using the road bridge to cross Aira Beck. After this, turn R along the signed public footpath which leads uphill from the side of a green-painted shed. The gate ahead, adjacent to Forge Mill, provides access to the National Trust land of Water Millock Common (Watermillock on the OLM). From here, a wide track leads further up the vast rounded, grassy fellsides, leading you SW. However, be careful to bear L off the main track before this dips to cross a watercourse. This critical turning is about 150 paces beyond the access gate and it changes your direction temporarily to SSW as you continue up the open fellside along a less distinct track, which follows the course of a tiny watercourse to your R leading towards higher ground ahead.

The next section of the way threads up through vast, open landscapes where behind you there are fine views down towards the cosy hamlet of Dockray, nestling snugly amongst a screen of protective trees. The path crosses the meandering watercourse further uphill at a point where it has become no more than a tiny, narrow water channel. From here the grassy slopes do steepen, but the compensation is that the path becomes better defined and consolidated as it continues to lead SW, gaining further height at a still comfortable rate. As you progress further uphill the irregular shape of Place Fell appears to the S, observed through the shallow hause ahead to your L.

The route now swings to the R more directly in line with the craggy features above, towards which progress is made along a broad path of tufted, coarse grasses. The gradient steepens progressively along here. The path-of-sorts divides in this area, before becoming better defined once again as you head SW up through a craggy area containing exposed rock. The first glimpses of Ullswater then appear way below on your L to the SE. These impressive sightings of the lake extend as further height is gained, and eventually most of its snaking length is revealed. The way then crosses an often boggy watercourse and rounds a grassy knoll rising to your R, before the narrow path of compacted earth skirts/connects with another way coming up on your L. This tracks parallel to a dry stone wall below you and the connecting path forms part of your descent route.

Now tackle the last grassy slopes which rise to your R to gain the summit of Common Fell. The final approach is across and up relatively steeply rising, grassy slopes, where the path is somewhat obscure in places and, paradoxically, easier to find and keep to during the first part of the way down. The advice is to head almost due W up the rising, grassy ground, selecting a way which avoids the very steepest sections and controls the rate of climb to one which is comfortable. You will then reach the summit cairn, standing on a fairly level and gently rounded area of ground, just after passing by an isolated large boulder.

Common Fell commands a height of 553m (1815ft) and is the highest point of the route. Allow yourself some time when you reach the rounded, grassy summit area to catch your breath and to observe the magnificent all-round panoramic views revealed in fine weather from this relatively isolated, elevated fell. A few of the highlights to be identified in the vast, rolling landscapes which stretch away in all directions are Skiddaw (NW); Blencathra (Saddleback) (NNW); the isolated, rounded hillock of Little Mell Fell and the distant Pennines (NE); Gowbarrow Fell (ENE); Ullswater writhing away down below (between E and ENE), with the high spurs of the easterly Fells climbing progressively higher to culminate in High Street far beyond Red Screes dominating the ground above Kirkstone Pass (S); St Sunday Crag leading your focus to the heights of Fairfield beyond (SSW); and Helvellyn, Catstye Cam and the Dodds (W).

Start your descent to the E veering ENE by walking past the large 'erratic' boulder which you passed on the way up, leaving this

16.2 The upper
falls above Aira
Force.

behind to your L. Trim your route to follow the easier, less steep, grassy slopes as you walk down the fellside following a faint track from which it is quite easy to stray temporarily, although this is not a problem. When the track bears L, abandon it by striking off across the beckoning, open fellside to maintain your primary easterly bearing. This course will lead you to a formidable dry stone wall below on your R. A clearer path is crossed at an acute angle as you descend to the wall, and when you reach it bear L to follow the direction of the walling further downhill, now walking NE to pass by the hillock of Round How to your L. The ground ahead tends to hold water, and following heavy rain there are muddy patches which necessitate the occasional slight detour.

Use the line of the wall on your R to guide you, never straying far from this as you continue your undulating descent. When you reach the place where the paths divide opt for the fork to the R, nearest to the faithful line of the wall, which you continue to track down beside. You will then reach another wall and wire fence running at right angles across your direction of approach. Turn R at the intersecting corner of the two walls, using a wooden stile to escape over the descending wall. Climb over this with some care, turning around at the top as there is no post against which to steady yourself and the stile is quite high. There is a rough, rocky descent from here along a path of sorts, close to the continuation of the stone wall. This is now on your L. The descent leads to another stile which again is awkward to get over, this one because of the steep fall-away on the far side.

134

The worst is now past, and a relatively easy section of path leads from here down to the quarry carpark located at MR 396211. Cross the A5091 road on a downwards diagonal and leave this through a gate positioned at the far end of the adjacent carparking layby, to return to the National Trust land of Gowbarrow. A clear, well-used path leads across the fields eastwards towards the tree-lined gully ahead. Pass through a swing gate and turn R along the grassy path signed to Lower Force – Pinetum. Bear further R to follow the rocky continuation path downstream. A really delightful stretch now follows above the course of Aira Beck, as it tumbles noisily towards Ullswater. Its progress is swift when cascading down numerous miniature waterfalls, and languid when temporarily trapped in small, deep catchment pools worn away at the bottom of each fall.

Lower down the route veers R away from a bridge crossing the stream, to continue some distance above the rushing waters which now spill through a narrow, rocky ravine over a boulder-strewn bed. The way down eventually reaches the higher of the two arched stone bridges, which you were recommended to venture on to some hours earlier. Do not cross this bridge, but instead bear R up the steps ahead. After this, a pleasant shaded path leads further down the wooded gorge to return you to the spot where you descended steeply down steps earlier in the day to reach the lower bridge. On this occasion, do not repeat the steep climb down but continue with your less exciting descent back to the carpark, now only a short distance further down the valley.

PLACES AND ACTIVITIES OF INTEREST

AIRA FORCE

Aira Force is situated below Gowbarrow Fell, near to the northern shoreline of Ullswater, about halfway along the lake. The spectacular waterfalls follow a fracture in the ancient volcanic rock formed about 60 million years ago. The forested area surrounding the falls is thought to have been part of a former deer park and the idyllic setting of the cascades has inspired many poets, writers and painters, including Wordsworth, Coleridge and William Green, to interpret its 'romantic setting'.

Aira Force is now in the care of the National Trust, and in addition to a variety of paths leading to, around and above the spectacular gorge and the impressive falling waters, there is a café open for most of the year, toilets with access for wheelchairs and a trail for the visually impaired.

135

17 HARTSOP AND BROTHERS WATER

STARTING/ FINISHING POINT
Carpark at the top end of Hartsop village OLM 5: MR 411½130.
The route passes by an alternative starting point at the nearby parking area at Cow Bridge (MR 403134)

GRADING OF WALK
Easy/ straightforward

TIME ALLOWANCE
1½ hours

DISTANCE
4.5km (2.8 miles)

TOTAL HEIGHT GAINED
35m (115ft)

HIGHEST POINT
Hartsop village 185m (605ft)

GRADIENTS
Occasional pleasant, gentle, short uphill stretches

PARKING
Small, unsurfaced carpark for 20-25 cars

PUBLIC TRANSPORT
CMS bus route 517 Bowness to Glenridding (The Kirkstone Rambler)

GENERAL
The paths and minor roads are good and route finding is easy

TACKLING THE WALK

CASUAL WALKERS

This walk is almost tailor made for the less ambitious walker. The route, if not necessarily the weather, is guaranteed to delight the most discerning rambler and, with no significant gradients to conquer, most walkers will be able to complete the circuit in a relatively short time should they choose to do so.

FAMILY WALKERS

This is an almost perfect route for walkers who have young children, although be warned that you might not get beyond Brothers Water! Still, you can always turn around and retrace your steps should your stay on the beach take up more time than expected.

DEDICATED FELL WALKERS

Strong walkers may prefer to combine this route with a more challenging walk into the surrounding high fells, of which there are numerous possibilities. Alternatively, it makes a grand evening stroll during the long days of summer, relaxing after dinner and an energetic day spent among the mountains. There is also the possibility of an early breakfast at the Barn End Bar.

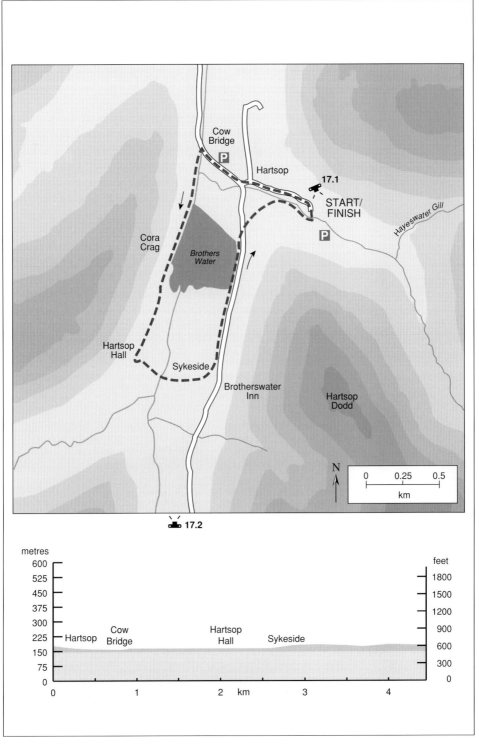

Cow
Bridge

Hartsop

17.1

START/
FINISH

Hayeswater Gill

Cora
Crag

*Brothers
Water*

Hartsop
Hall

Sykeside

Brotherswater
Inn

Hartsop
Dodd

N

| 0 | 0.25 | 0.5 |

km

17.2

metres					feet
600					1800
525					
450					1500
375					1200
300		Cow	Hartsop		900
225	Hartsop	Bridge	Hall	Sykeside	600
150					
75					300
0					0

| 0 | 1 | 2 | km | 3 | 4 |

ARTSOP village is quite superbly located beneath the towering fells of The Knott to the E, Gray Crag to the ESE and Hartsop Dodd to the S. However, your route leads away from these mighty fells, back through the village of Hartsop and along the narrow access lane, taking you NW to the main A592 road at MR 405132. The village is very picturesque, the rightful pride and joy of its caring residents, and its attractive stone cottages with their gardens crammed full of colourful flowers make it a particularly pleasing starting location for the walk. Beyond the buildings, the route leads beside a stream gurgling merrily away on your L. This contains the combined catchment waters of Hayswater Gill and Pasture Beck. Just before reaching the main road you will pass the Langton Adventure Centre, with an adjacent side road off to your R which you ignore.

Turn R along the main road in the direction of Patterdale, using the pavement on your side of the road to continue NW down the flat valley. The grassy hillsides now on your R are part of the extensive slopes rising to Place Fell, which overlooks Ullswater from the SE. Given favourable weather, over to your rear and L, you will be able to observe the long, craggy spurs culminating in the heights of High Hartsop Dodd, Middle Dodd and Red Screes to the SSW. A short distance further on, cross the busy road with care before veering L

17.1 Hartsop and Gray Crag.

towards the alternative parking area beyond which the refreshing waters of Goldrill Beck are crossed by means of a hump-backed stone bridge. This is at a particularly pleasant, shaded spot.

Turn L on the far side of the stream to pass through a K-gate on your L. This provides entrance to the National Trust Hartsop Hall farmlands. The Hall is over 400 years old and there is an interesting information sign telling you about this at the access point. Through the gate, keep to the broad gravel path which leads up the valley just above the stream, ignoring all side paths up the steep fellside on your R. The way is under a delightful canopy of deciduous foliage during the summer months and the leaves of beech, oak and sycamore provide welcome shade. Your direction is now S, directly towards Brothers Water, which soon appears ahead to your L.

There is a shingle beech located just beyond the exit stream from the lake a short distance below your path, and this usually proves irresistible to younger children. You can continue southwards along this for some distance before being forced to rejoin the main path just above. The views across the tarn from here on fine, sunny days are a joy to behold. Beyond the clear, intense blue of Brothers Water, steep green slopes lead the eye towards the grey and brown mountains above, which are linked together by perfectly proportioned connecting ridges. In fine weather the separate peaks of The Knott (E), Grey Crag (ESE), Hartsop Dodd (SE), Stony Cove Pike (SSE), Kirkstone Pass (S) and High Hartsop Dodd and Red Screes (SSW) may all be identified.

When you have to rejoin the main path, do this along a narrow traverse and then veer L to walk further S around the tarn, where you will be rewarded by further fine views. These are observed through convenient gaps in nearby foliage on your L. Progress along the wide, secure path is swift and most enjoyable. This section of the walk through broadleaved woodlands terminates towards the southern tip of the lake, where you emerge close to more grass-fringed beaches.

The path maintains its elevated course southwards past the tarn and along the flat, glaciated valley towards Hartsop Hall. A K-gate (tight squeeze) is negotiated *en route* to the Hall, followed by a second one positioned near to the buildings. Walk around the Hall, keeping this to your L. Continue to bear further L to avoid following the continuation path directly up the valley, to reach and follow the wide track which heads first SE and then E across the valley floor, back towards the main road. Pass through a gate positioned to the R of a cattle grid and use the track and bridge to cross Kirkstone Beck at MR 399½119. After this, another K-gate to the L of a second cattle grid provides access to the well-appointed campsite at Sykeside.

17.2 Brothers Water spied from the Kirkstone Pass.

Walk through the campsite keeping to the surfaced driveway, and exit up the brow on your L.This will lead you past the Barn End Bar, where you may purchase breakfast. Continue walking up the slope, but be careful to bear further L before you reach the Brotherswater Inn, above to your R. In completing these last manoeuvres your direction will have changed towards NNE and you will now be heading back down the valley towards Brothers Water. Just before reaching the main road, branch off along the narrow National Trust permissive footpath, which leads through a wooden gate in the direction of the lake.

After crossing a small stream by a slate slab, you will quickly reach the tarn again by passing through more deciduous wood-land, this time containing a pleasing mixture of beech, birch, hazel, rowan and sycamore. On your way to the tarn you have to pass through a wide gap in the stone walling on your R for the very briefest of encounters with the road, before a continuation stretch of pathway obligingly descends away from this busy traffic artery. This quick escape leads you back towards the more tranquil setting of the blue lake, its surface here covered with white water-lilies.

Your return path winds around the eastern shoreline of Brothers Water, meandering near to the edge of the water under a thick canopy of overhanging foliage. The way leads all too soon to your departure point from the tarn, where beyond another K-gate there are more opportunities to rest, picnic and splash about by the edge of the water. The path then rises up the grassy bank on your R to pass through another K-gate before reaching the road again. This connection is at MR 406128. Cross the road carefully, selecting a diagonal to your L, and then turn off R up the grassy brow ahead. Following this, turn almost immediately L again along the signed public footpath, which is accessed through a wooden gate.

From here, a pleasant narrow, stony path leads NNE, climbing marginally uphill around the slope on your R. Ahead, bear further R towards Hartsop, the buildings of which soon reappear ahead. An obvious way threads through the first of these and when you approach the beck bear R, keeping to the higher ground to avoid crossing the stream by the concrete bridge down on your L. Pass through the wooden gate bearing the sign 'Footpath' and proceed up the valley following a wide, stony path which leads above the stream on your L. Pass through another wooden gate and then turn L in order to cross the beck where, after passing through two more gates, the second a K-gate, the carpark is reached on your L.

PLACES AND ACTIVITIES OF INTEREST

HARTSOP

This really delightful village is situated up a side valley from Patterdale to the E of Brothers Water. It is an extremely popular starting venue for tackling the easterly fells, including walking along the former Roman communication route over High Street. You will need to be self-sufficient in food and drink, because the tiny hamlet does not have any commercial refreshment facilities.

BROTHERS WATER

This natural lake was gouged out by powerful glacial action during successive Ice Ages. Since then, the lake has been continuously infilled with sediment relentlessly brought down by the feeding waters of Kirkstone Beck, which accounts for its present shallowness. The lake supports reeds and rushes which provide ideal shelter for the ducks, coots and other waterfowl which frequent its waters. Fishermen also praise the quality of the trout which provide sport for them here.

AROUND
CONISTON

18 TARN HOWS AND BLACK CRAG

**STARTING/
FINISHING POINT**
Carpark at the sw
tip of Tarn Hows
OLM 7: MR
327995½

**GRADING OF
WALK**
Moderate/
challenging

TIME ALLOWANCE
2½ hours

DISTANCE
6.7km (4.2 miles)

**TOTAL HEIGHT
GAINED**
170m (560ft)

HIGHEST POINT
Black Crag
322m (1055ft)

GRADIENTS

From the N end of the tarn to the summit of Black Crag is mostly uphill, but there are only a few steep slopes and these are well spaced out. The most demanding section is the final approach to the craggy summit

PARKING

Extensive, well-screened but very popular National Trust parking facilities. Separate parking for disabled visitors nearby at MR 330995

PUBLIC TRANSPORT

Not on a bus route

GENERAL

The paths are mostly good and clear, with rougher ground towards the summit of Black Crag

TACKLING THE WALK

CASUAL WALKERS

This is an ideal route for all those who wish to gain a taste of the fells and of walking across some open terrain, but who do not relish either severe gradients or complicated route finding. There is also the added bonus of walking around Tarn Hows as a preliminary to the main objective rather than as the sole attraction.

FAMILY WALKERS

This walk is quite suitable for most family groups and it will be only the very young who experience any significant difficulty in reaching the summit of Black Crag. The alternative is simply to opt for a leisurely stroll around Tarn Hows, stopping occasionally to splash about by the water's edge.

DEDICATED FELL WALKERS

Most serious explorers of the Lakeland Fells will have walked round Tarn Hows many times, but relatively few will have stood on

Previous pages:
*The colourful
approach to
Brantwood from
the jetty.*

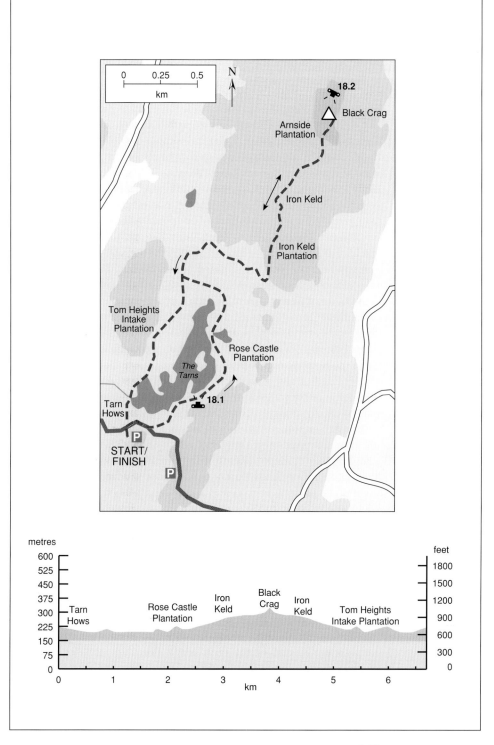

START/
FINISH

the top of Black Crag. If this is true in your case then try the walk, perhaps during a fine evening, for it is almost certain that not only will you be impressed by what you observe from this commanding viewing position but you will also enjoy getting there and back.

B EFORE starting the actual circuit itself, scale the higher ground to the E of the parking area to obtain a splendid view looking N across the irregular, indented shape of Tarn Hows nestling below within a pleasant wooded area of mature pines. In clear weather you can also see the Langdale Pikes (NNW), Fairfield and Helvellyn (NNE), Red Screes and Ill Bell (NE), Coniston Old Man (WSW) and Wetherlam (WNW) from this elevated position. In addition, part of Coniston Water may be glimpsed to the SSW.

Descend northwards towards Tarn Hows and cross the single-track road before selecting one of the several paths which will lead you towards the water, following a downwards diagonal to your R to commence your anti-clockwise circuit of the tarn. Progress now is to the NE, where a short distance further on several smaller paths consolidate into the main, wide gravel path around the tarn. The clear and extremely pleasant way then passes through a system of gates before continuing to lead you above the indented shoreline of the tarn. Along this stretch there are opportunities to drop down to the edge of the water and follow the shore for some distance along one of several side paths, before reconnecting with the main path weaving around above the tarn.

Further on, bear L when you reach a definite branch path leading down towards the tarn. This wide path is composed of stone and gravel and leads beneath lofty conifers. This route, nearest to Tarn Hows, then leads past a tiny, almost hidden side tarn off to your R, the surface of which is smothered with water-lilies during the summer months. The detour to observe this tranquil scene, complete with summer house, is no more than a few paces. The path then becomes somewhat rougher for a short distance as it threads over exposed rock and crosses the exit stream from the side tarn. A better path soon becomes re-established, however, and this tracks around several inlets, leading through more pine trees. There are numerous secluded, shaded spots along here by the water's edge which make ideal picnic places.

This side track then connects with the main path once more, towards the NE end of the tarn. Bear L along this path and a short distance further on you will round the N tip of Tarn Hows, the path bridging several small feeder streams flowing into the tarn. In this area there is an unusual curved wooden form bearing the inscription '1927 PP 1991'. Be careful of the powerful spring-loaded K-gate, and beyond this trap keep to the obvious main track, avoiding all distracting side paths leading off to both L and R, until you reach a signed intersection of ways.

Turn R at this junction along the path signed to Arnside and Langdales. This will lead you northwards through mixed woodlands away from Tarn Hows to a gate and adjacent stile bridging a dry stone wall. This is the boundary of the National Trust lands; over the stile, turn R to head uphill along a broad, stony track which bisects the rising wooded fellsides. It is quite a pull up the slope, so take your time. The route then levels off temporarily and, about 250 paces after passing a gate through which you are informed that there is 'No Public Access', turn L to follow the signed public bridleway leading through the Iron Keld conifer plantation. Beyond a gate and stile a broad, stony path leads further uphill along a shallow incline. This allows you to make further progress to the N beneath the cooling shade of densely packed conifer trees. The uphill walk through the plantation covers about 0.5km (⅓ mile), after which open country is again reached at another gate-and-stile combination, this one located at MR 337011.

Emerging from the trees, follow the obvious main continuation path for a short distance to pass through a redundant gateway.

18.1 Early-morning stillness at Tarn Hows.

Immediately after this, at a cairn, select the path leading more steeply uphill on your R, which initially leads off backwards at an acute angle to your direction of approach. From here, another firm path leads NNE along a way marked by guiding cairns towards the horizon above. In continuing towards this, you will have to cross the occasional damp patch. The obvious path climbs up bracken-covered slopes, and as additional height is gained more distant landscapes come into view, which get better and better as you approach the summit area above.

The path leads to the craggy helmet of the isolated fell named Black Crag. In clear weather the all-round views from here are simply stunning. Although this peak commands only a modest height of 322m (1055ft), the fell has immense stature, and distant landscapes may be admired from it in almost every direction. Start by looking NW, where beyond Little Langdale and Lingmoor Fell the mighty slopes of Pike of Blisco, Crinkle Crags, Bow Fell and the Langdale Pikes compete for your attention. Then, rotating clockwise, identify Helvellyn and the Fairfield Horseshoe (N), Red Screes (NNE), part of the E fells dominated by the pointed peak of Ill Bell (ENE), a large portion of Windermere with the Pennines far beyond (E), Esthwaite Water and Hawkshead (SSE), Coniston and Tarn Hows (SSW) and the massive fellsides of Coniston Old Man and Wetherlam (SW). What a fantastic and varied panorama.

The descent retraces your approach steps back to the junction of ways near to the N end of Tarn Hows at MR 331006. However, before you commence this descent to the SSW, undertake a short diversion over the L-stile on your R and use the permissive, grassy way to reach a second magnificent viewing platform. This is a rocky mound located a short distance to the N of the summit of Black Crag and marked on the OLM as being 1m (3ft) higher! Do not venture any further along the grassy path, which then leads downhill, but instead return to the summit area of Black Crag, having recrossed the L-stile to get there, and then begin your descent towards Tarn Hows.

When you reach the junction of ways (MR 331006), continue more or less straight ahead to walk S along the path signed 'Coniston and Carpark around Tarn'. Further delightful views across the sheltered waters of Tarn Hows await you ahead, these now to the E and seen through gaps in the intervening foliage. The way soon reaches more open terrain where on clear, windless, sunny days the less restricted views across the tarn are superb. The return path crosses a man-made dam towards the SW tip of the tarn and then passes through the adjacent K-gate, where a choice of paths then leads up the grassy slopes ahead to cover the short distance back to the parking area.

PLACES AND ACTIVITIES OF INTEREST

*18.2 Approaching
the summit of
Black Crag from
the north.*

TARN HOWS

This delightful man-made tarn, which flooded and joined together
three smaller, natural stretches of water, is a Mecca for walkers and
general tourists alike. Its great appeal is due to several factors: lying
a short distance to the NE of Coniston, it is easy to reach by road;
there are good parking facilities, the wide, undulating paths around
the tarn, accessible by wheelchair, present easy, pleasant walking;
given good weather, the views of the surrounding fells are quite
magnificent; and the attractively shaped tarn, nestling within
conifer-covered slopes, supports a wide range of wildlife, of which
the flying and/or swimming variety predominate.

The sheltered tarn is hidden by folded fells at an altitude of just
below 200m (600ft) and it has a maximum depth of approaching
10m (30ft). The tarn and its surroundings are now in the care of
the National Trust due to the generosity of Beatrix Potter, who
bequeathed the property to the Trust in 1943.

A few words of caution: it is extremely tempting to swim in
these waters on a hot summer's day or to tread on the ice when the
surface of the tarn is frozen over. The only sensible advice is refrain
from both, due to the inherent danger of getting into difficulties or
even drowning at this seemingly benign spot.

149

19 *GONDOLA*, BRANTWOOD AND CRAG HEAD

**STARTING/
FINISHING POINT**
Boat pier at
Coniston. OLM 5:
MR 308969½.
Walk starts and
finishes at
Brantwood
MR 313958½.

**GRADING OF
WALK**
Easy/
straightforward

TIME ALLOWANCE
1½ hours

DISTANCE
2.1km (1.3 miles)

**TOTAL HEIGHT
GAINED**
140m (460ft)

HIGHEST POINT
Crag Head
230m (755ft)

GRADIENTS

The way from Brantwood to the summit of Crag Head is all uphill. Some sections are quite steep and relatively demanding, but the entire climb is moderately short

PARKING

The extensive parking areas near the pier are free and therefore extremely popular. There are nearby toilets, and refreshments at the Blue Bird Café

PUBLIC TRANSPORT

CMS bus route 505/506 (The Coniston Rambler) through Coniston village, a short distance from the lake, connecting Bowness, Windermere, Ambleside, Coniston, Hawkshead and Hilltop

GENERAL

The excellent Nature Trails in Brantwood Estate are not public rights of way and a modest usage charge may be levied to help fund their upkeep. The way to and from the top of Crag Head demands a little more concentration on route finding

TACKLING THE WALK

CASUAL WALKERS

This is an ideal walk for most reasonably fit walkers who do not mind a bit of climbing, providing they are under no pressure to complete it in record time. There is no hurry, providing you catch an early sailing and have the greater part of the day at your disposal, so pace yourself and spend plenty of time admiring the superb views down over Coniston Water.

FAMILY WALKERS

The boat trip on *Gondola*, the many attractions of Brantwood, and the nature trails through its extensive grounds and woodlands are a must for most family visitors. How far you get up towards Crag Head is your choice, but one of the many attributes of this walk is

150

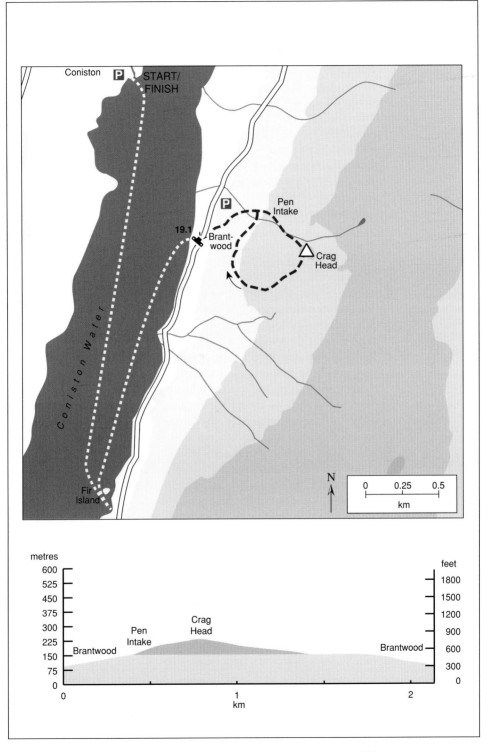

Coniston
START/
FINISH

Pen
Intake

Brant-
wood

19.1

Crag
Head

Coniston Water

Fir
Island

N

0   0.25   0.5

km

metres

600
525
450
375
300
225
150
75
0

Crag
Head

Pen
Intake

Brantwood

Brantwood

feet

1800
1500
1200
900
600
300
0

0   1   2
km

151

that when you have had enough you can return to the delights at Brantwood or take the children down to play along the attractive shoreline of Coniston Water.

DEDICATED FELL WALKERS

If you have never stood on the summit of Crag Head – as many committed fell explorers may not have done – do so now, for you will not be disappointed. Should you wish to explore further there is a maze of extensions through the conifer plantations above, and you may like to plan a route using the forest paths and tracks above Crag Head to reach Carron Crag to the SSE, returning to Brantwood from here by a longer, more circuitous route through Lawson Park. Remember to watch the time carefully, though, so that you do not miss your return sailing.

THIS walk will have to be timed to fit in with the scheduled sailings of the steam yacht *Gondola*. Try to allow a minimum of at least three hours or so between your outward and return trips. The interior fittings of *Gondola* are luxurious, and because on a fine, warm windless day the sail down Coniston Water is sublime, with a great deal to see, it is a good idea to board the yacht well before it sails and have a good look around down below so that you can spend the entire trip up on deck sightseeing.

As the yacht glides out across Coniston Water, the massive fellsides rising to Coniston Old Man can be observed to your R rearing above the shingle bays and woodlands fringing the westerly shoreline of the lake. On the other, E side of the lake, densely forested slopes surround the extensive clearing in which Ruskin's former residence – the white-painted Brantwood – is located.

The relaxing boat trip takes you down the lake well past Brantwood on its outward journey as far as the jetty at Park-A-Moor, which is set in an attractive, sheltered bay. During this 45-minute sail s the rugged grandeur of the surrounding landscapes gradually diminishes as the narrow lake penetrates more rounded, lower fellsides. From Park-A-Moor the yacht backtracks up the lake to reach the landing stage serving Brantwood. During the summer months, the short walk up to the house is a delight, passing through a garden crammed with shrubs and other plants, their swaying flowers cascading in brilliant patterns.

Turn L when you reach the road, passing by the Coach House Gallery and Jumping Jenny Tearooms on your R before reaching Brantwood. The lower part of the climb to the summit of Crag Head makes use of part of the extensive nature trails threading through the grounds of Brantwood. Start by climbing up the flight of steps to the R of the entrance to the house, to enter Brantwood

Estate. You will pass an interesting Ruskin exhibition hall immediately on your L.

When the path ahead forks, select the higher L branch and pass through a wooden gate before branching L again to ascend steeper ground, passing The Old-Fashioned Penthouse *en route*. Climb the steps ahead and bear R along a terraced path before climbing more steps. Then veer L along a wide path which leads through deciduous woodland, gaining height up the fellside under refreshing shade. Along this elevated stretch there are tantalizing glimpses of Coniston Water and the Coniston Fells through the occasional gap in the foliage down to your L.

At a point where your wide track curves to the L and begins to descend, select the narrow continuation path which leads through bracken off to the R and then follow this around as it curves L. The following section of the nature trail is quite superb, passing through magnificent, airy woodland where the less densely packed trees allow shafts of light to penetrate and support lush ground vegetation. Your forfeit for this is that you have to carry on climbing, albeit up a more comfortable gradient along a clear and firm narrow path. The way continues to lead you uphill along a series of graceful curves.

Higher up, pass through a K-gate and cross over the track where trail marker 18 is positioned, to continue further uphill along the obvious extension of your approach path. Another uphill section follows, but there is a terrific payback for your efforts when you emerge from the woodland into more open terrain. Here, quite suddenly, clear, unrestricted views appear between W and NNW of Coniston Water and the majestic amphitheatre of the Coniston Fells rising beyond the lake. The separate peaks of Coniston Old Man, Swirl How and Wetherlam are all revealed. A little higher up still, be careful to follow the main path as it swings to the R before curving back up steps further on.

You then reach more open fellsides, which signals that the climbing is nearly over. Having passed trail marker 17, there is just one remaining bracken-clad, craggy knoll separating you from the summit cairn (and trail marker 16) of Crag Head. This fell commands a height of 230m (755ft) and is the highest point of the walk. In clear weather, the views from here are stunning. Those to the W down towards Coniston Water and beyond of the Coniston Fells are already familiar to you. However, there are also compelling new vistas of the Langdale Pikes to the N, and Helvellyn and Fairfield to the NNE.

Start your descent to the SSW along the obvious extension of the circular trail to the summit of Crag Head, initially coming down through extensive areas of bracken. Trail markers 15, 14 and 13 are quickly left above as you make use of helpfully positioned duckboards placed to span the occasional muddy patch straddling the path in wet conditions. The obvious way down converges on a wide track below, along which you turn R. This continuation way then traverses lower down the bracken-covered fellside, losing height at an appreciably slower rate. Further on, you re-enter the extensive woodlands of Crag Coppice.

The return route leads you back to the K-gate and trail marker 18. Turn L and pass through this gate to complete the higher-level loop of the walk. From here, either retrace your outward steps back to Brantwood or lower down select one of the alternative trails through the woodlands. When you get down, there may still be time for you to complete your tour of the house and gardens and perhaps even take some well-earned refreshment at the Jumping Jenny, before tackling the short distance back to the jetty to await the arrival of the *Gondola*.

PLACES AND ACTIVITIES OF INTEREST

19.1 Waiting for   **STEAM YACHT *GONDOLA***
the approaching   The refurbished steam yacht *Gondola* is the rightful pride and
Gondola *at*   joy of the National Trust. Their brochure invites you to cruise
Brantwood.   on Coniston Water in Victorian style, travelling in opulently

upholstered and spacious saloons, which on this occasion is an understatement. The yacht can carry up to 86 passengers and she cruises, apparently effortlessly, at up to 8½ knots, which is the speed limit on the lake. She was originally launched from Coniston Hall for service on Coniston Water in 1859 and since then has had a colourful history, including having her original boiler sold to power a saw mill, and being used as a houseboat.

There are sailings every day from the end of March to the beginning of November, and the circular trip is from Coniston pier down to Park-A-Moor pier (opposite Torver), with the return loop via Brantwood jetty. Unfortunately, the trip is not suitable for those in wheelchairs, and be warned that there are no toilet facilities on board. However, party bookings and private charters are possible.

*For further details or to obtain a timetable, contact National Trust (Enterprises) Ltd, *Gondola* bookings (see Useful Addresses).*

CONISTON LAUNCH

From Coniston pier there is an alternative, less sumptuous but still extremely appealing way of sailing to Brantwood. This is by means of the scheduled ferry service operated by Coniston Launch, which supplements the more opulent *Gondola* sailings. The service is provided by two traditional Lakes launches, *Ruskin* and *Ransome*, built in the 1920s. Private charters are also offered on these launches and there are special-interest cruises, including Nautical Nostalgia and Campbells on Coniston.

For further details or to obtain a timetable, contact Coniston Launch (see Useful Addresses, contact telephone numbers).

BRANTWOOD

Brantwood, John Ruskin's home from 1872 to 1900, is open to visitors throughout the year. Perched below woodlands on the E shores of Coniston Water, the house became an intellectual focus and one of the premier literary and artistic centres in Europe. When you visit it, you may like to consider that Tolstoy, Mahatma Gandhi, Marcel Proust and Frank Lloyd Wright were among many inspired by Ruskin.

Brantwood still has a very special atmosphere, and the house, gardens and extensive fellside grounds should have something to appeal to all visitors, be they in hiking boots or high heels. The house contains a collection of Ruskin's superb drawings, watercolours and memorabilia, plus a fine bookshop. There are extensive nature trails through the surrounding grounds and woodland gardens, Ruskin Lace demonstrations every Thursday in season, special exhibitions and events, and quite outstanding refreshment facilities at the Jumping Jenny Tearooms, which also stage musical evenings.

For further information, contact Brantwood and Jumping Jenny Tearooms (see Useful Addresses).

20 TORVER BACK COMMON, CONISTON WATER AND MILL BRIDGE

**STARTING/
FINISHING POINT**
Parking area off the
A5084, to the s of
Torver opposite
Lakeland Land
Rover Garage
OLM 6: MR
287½932

**GRADING OF
WALK**
Easy/
straightforward

TIME ALLOWANCE
3 hours

DISTANCE
5.8km (3.6 miles)

**TOTAL HEIGHT
GAINED**
205m (670ft)

HIGHEST POINT
Torver Back
Common
150m (490ft)

GRADIENTS

Some climbing is involved, but the slopes are not particularly challenging and the uphill sections are well spaced out along gradual inclines

PARKING

The parking area is up a rough, unmade slope with space for 10–15 cars on sloping ground. There is alternative parking nearby adjacent to the road

PUBLIC TRANSPORT

Not on a bus route

GENERAL

The paths are mixed, varying from clear to indistinct and crossing both firm and soft ground, with some boggy stretches. The Cumbrian Way along Coniston Water is rough and stony. Careful route finding is required across Torver Back Common

TACKLING THE WALK

CASUAL WALKERS

This is a fine route for less ambitious walkers who enjoy the freedom of the open fells, with a section of more sheltered lakeside walking thrown in for good measure. The route should be ideal for all moderately capable walkers, in terms of both their fitness and route-finding expertise.

FAMILY WALKERS

The walk is suitable for those with older children. Family groups with younger children may prefer to spend their time wandering about Torver Back Common, investigating more thoroughly the tarns and their contents hidden away among the folded fells of the higher ground, and avoiding the more exacting descent to and subsequent climb back from Coniston Water.

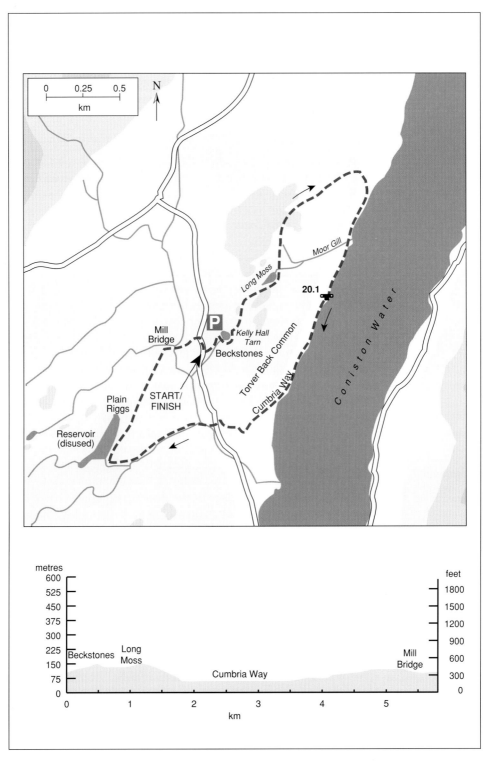

0   0.25   0.5
km

N

Moor Gill

Long Moss

20.1

P

Mill
Bridge

Kelly Hall
Tarn

Beckstones

Torver Back Common

Cumbria Way

Coniston Water

Plain
Riggs

START/
FINISH

Reservoir
(disused)

metres
600
525
450
375
300
225
150
75
0

feet
1800
1500
1200
900
600
300
0

Beckstones

Long
Moss

Cumbria Way

Mill
Bridge

0   1   2   3   4   5
km

DEDICATED FELL WALKERS

There are plenty of opportunities for extending this walk either along Torver Back Common or alternatively further north-westwards to loop in Torver with its enticing inns. In favourable weather the views are continuously outstanding, and for this reason this route, or an extension thereof, should find favour with most energetic walkers.

OLLOW the rough track leading NE up the fell from the top end of the parking area. This is to the R of the Lakeland Land Rover Garage parking lot. The way leads to a K-gate positioned beneath a mountain ash tree, which provides convenient access to the open ground of Torver Back Common. Bear L from here, continuing to gain height along a broad, grassy track which leads towards the corner of a stone wall ahead. In clear weather there are now magnificent views of the Coniston Fells and the separate peaks of Brown and Buck Pikes, Dow Crag and Coniston Old Man, which may all be distinguished to the NNW. When in bloom, nearby gorse bushes provide the perfect foreground for photographs of these impressive fells.

The continuation track leads you almost immediately to a small reeded tarn. This is Kelly Hall Tarn and a leisurely (anti-clockwise) amble around it to observe the marginal plants and wildlife is recommended. From the higher ground beyond the tiny exit stream there are more majestic views of the Coniston Fells, now observed across the tranquil waters of the small tarn in which, on still days, reflections of a group of trees may be observed. Continue circling the tarn, taking in your stride a patch of often, squelchy, water-logged ground and passing by a 'No Swimming' notice, until you reconnect with a continuation of the grassy path which you abandoned to walk around the tarn. Turn acutely to the R along this and follow it as it winds further up the fell.

The track soon becomes significantly less distinct as you endeavour to follow it, walking NE veering N and still gaining height. The next part of the way follows a shallow depression which passes rocky outcrops to your immediate L. Fortunately, a short distance further on the path becomes considerably better defined again as it leads to the higher ground to the W of another certain landmark. This is a narrow strip of trapped water, appropriately named Long Moss Tarn. Long Moss also supports reeds and other water plants, and it lies below to your R. You then reach an even better-established, narrow path running at right angles to your approach. Turn R along this, changing your bearing to NE to walk towards Coniston Water as you follow the elevated path above the tiny tarn.

From here, when the weather is fine it is possible to see the far-away Fairfield Fells across the tarn to the NNE. Then, more directly ahead, part of Coniston Water comes into view, a considerable distance below. Walk to the pointed E tip of Long Moss Tarn to observe the splendid vista to the NE across the tranquil waters choked with reeds, bog bean and other plants. It is important now to resist the obvious temptation to continue due E directly towards Coniston Water beside the exit stream of Moor Gill, as this leads to some rough, steep fellsides with no adequate continuation through paths down to the lake. Instead, depart along the broad grassy path leading NNE, keeping for the time being to the higher ground as the way winds up a further modest, bracken-covered slope directly ahead.

At the base of the next, often boggy, hollow be careful to bear R, keeping to the grassy way and ignoring a stony path leading uphill to your L. Skirt around the often boggy ground in this vicinity (to the R is usually the favoured course), but within a few paces again be vigilant to bear L in order to cross a stony watercourse, before heading up the craggy brow ahead. Still track to the L, to locate a clearer path which then climbs up the more pronounced slope ahead, tracking NE. Your way then connects with an alternative path up from the waterlogged dell and you bear R along this combined and much clearer wide, grassy path leading NE. The worst of the route-finding challenges are now behind you.

Safely over the next shallow rise, it is all downhill towards Coniston Water. The descent to the NE aligns with a prominent white-painted house on the far side of the lake; this is Brantwood, John Ruskin's home from 1872 to 1900 (see Walk 19). The clear and obvious path, into which other routes funnel to consolidate the way down, divides for a short distance further down. However, either branch may be chosen for the two paths converge again quite quickly. The advice is to choose the path to the L, nearest to the shallow gully and miniature watercourse, but be careful not to cross these features. Instead, constantly select branch paths which follow the stream down along its R bank. This keeps you to the main descent route on your now established NE bearing.

Lower down, veer R away from the beck along a wider track. This winds further down the fellside, leading through a gate to enter a wooded area, predominantly of oak. Continue to descend, now in the shade of Torver Common Wood which is very welcome on hot, sunny days. Branch R further on to complete the final part of your descent to Coniston Water along a broad, winding path which leads down on a diagonal to the SE. Walk right to the stony beach below for an unrestricted view across the lake, before continuing southwards along the shoreline path. This is part of the Cumbria Way.

As you continue tracking down the lake, particularly on still days during the winter months when the surface of the water is perfectly calm, your thoughts might turn to the exploits of Donald Campbell and his courageous but ill-fated attempt in *Bluebird* to break the 300 mile-per-hour barrier on Coniston Water and thus recapture the world water-speed record for Britain. The stony path leading southwards along the tree-fringed shoreline climbs over a series of unexacting undulations, including one higher, craggy knoll, and this pattern continues for the next 2km (1¼ miles) or so. There are more temptations along here in the form of sheltered bays with stony beaches, as the rough path leads past Moor Gill Foot and Bellman's Hole, features shown on the OLM.

In continuing southwards under silver birch trees and through clumps of gorse bushes, always keep to the paths nearest to the lake, studiously avoiding all side paths leading up the steep fellside to your R. Keep a careful eye on any younger children in your party along here, and also keep a tight grip on their wrists when you have to pass the few sections which feature potentially dangerous drops down rocky pitches to your L. The way passes through an isolated K-gate and just before reaching a stone boat house the continuation path rises, turning westwards away from Coniston Water.

The rising route leads to and then follows the line of a stone wall, which encloses more deciduous woodlands to your L. Further up the path fans out in several directions, and here your route is along the more eroded, rocky path which leads due W almost directly ahead, taking you towards a stone wall and a clump of trees higher up. A wider, more level path then circles around the brow of the fellside beside another stone wall, this one to your R. Pass through the K-gate ahead and continue circling around to the R to pass almost immediately beneath overhead electricity cables. Views of the Coniston Fells reappear at this point, as does part of your continuation route up the grassy slopes on the far side of Torver Beck.

Follow the obvious path down to the A5084 road and cross this on a diagonal to your L to locate the footpath leading off almost directly opposite towards Torver Low Common. This is accessed through a K-gate. The route then crosses the foaming white waters of Torver Beck at a safe height by means of a secure, wooden footbridge. A grassy path winds westwards from the far side of the beck, leading up the bracken-covered fellside. Further on, be careful to keep L when the path forks to continue W up a shallow, tree-lined gully through which a small stream flows. This remote, narrow side valley gains height along a comfortable gradient.

A rocky path then bends to the R away from the trench and when this also forks ahead keep L, following the more grassy way which crosses a tiny watercourse before leading you towards the rocky outcrop above. Bear R to recross the watercourse, and then

veer L again to reach the eastern shore of the disused reservoir on Torver Low Common. Bear R here to walk NNE along this attractive elongated strip of water, gaining some additional height. The wide, open landscapes hereabouts are wild, barren, remote and majestic, and if you meet another soul when trekking this way you will be particularly unlucky!

20.1 Looking south down the pebbly shoreline of Coniston Water.

The wide, rutted path continues to wind up the fellside, gaining additional height above the reservoir which is now a considerable distance below you. Further on, keep to the main path which continues to lead northwards, ignoring a side path on your R which winds to the top of the nearby fell, named Anne Riggs. Given good weather, the open panorama to the N towards the now familiar profile of the Coniston Fells is quite outstanding. A wide grassy path then winds downhill, bearing R beside a stone wall to your R. Pass through the gate, also on the R, towards the bottom of the slope, continuing to descend along a now enclosed stony path. This leads down to the quaint huddle of buildings situated at Mill Bridge. Bear R again at this point, away from the continuation bridlepath signed to Torver off on your L. Cross Torver Beck again and then turn L to proceed uphill, passing through a gate in the process. An enclosed stony path then leads back to the A5084 road again at Emlin Hall. Finally, turn R to walk the short distance back to Beckstones and the carpark.

PLACES AND ACTIVITIES OF INTEREST

KELLY HALL AND LONG MOSS TARNS

These two contrasting tarns, hidden away among the complicated, folded fellsides of Torver Back Common, lie above and to the w of Coniston Water.

Kelly Hall Tarn is circular in shape and nestles down within bracken-covered fellsides, its shallow waters no more than a metre or two deep, supporting reeds and other pond life. The name is apparently derived from a former nearby building, but nowadays its main claim to fame are the superb views across its placid waters towards the distant Coniston Fells.

Long Moss Tarn reveals all in its name, because it is elongated in shape and its surface occupies a wet, moss-covered basin. The sheltered tarn supports reeds, bog bean, cotton grass and water-lilies, and this habitat is frequented by a wide variety of visiting birds and insects, including droning dragonflies during the summer months. Again, the views across the tarn are delightful when the sun is shining brightly, and those towards the sw from its eastern tip are among the very best.

SOUTHERN LAKELAND

21 GRIZEDALE FOREST PARK AND ESTHWAITE WATER

**STARTING/
FINISHING POINT**
Grizedale Forest
Visitor Centre, SW of
Hawkshead OLM 7:
MR 336944

**GRADING OF
WALK**
Moderate/
challenging

TIME ALLOWANCE
3 hours

DISTANCE
6.7km (4.2 miles)

**TOTAL HEIGHT
GAINED**
225m (735ft)

HIGHEST POINT
Forest heights
210m (690ft)

GRADIENTS
The slopes through the forested areas are not too severe, and the uphill sections are well spaced out at the beginning and towards the end of the route

PARKING
Large, well laid-out parking areas with extensive facilities including toilets, a café and the attractions of the Visitor Centre

PUBLIC TRANSPORT
Limited summer bus service 515 from Ambleside to Grizedale Forest Visitor Centre

GENERAL
The paths are very good for most of the way, although the forest roads do become churned up and muddy during harvesting and planting operations. You will need to be careful with route finding in a few places

TACKLING THE WALK

CASUAL WALKERS
This is an almost perfect walk for the less ambitious walker. There is plenty of interest along the way, with the delights of the Grizedale Forest Visitor Centre at both ends of the energetic part.

FAMILY WALKERS
The walk is suitable for most children above the age of about six or seven. Families who love the great outdoors are almost bound to delight in the many attractions of the Visitor Centre, and the biggest problem may be getting started on the walk at all.

DEDICATED FELL WALKERS
A visit to the Visitor Centre and a walk through the forest should appeal to most walkers, including the most energetic. There are many possibilities for extending the route and these may be

Previous page:
*Reflections on
Esthwaite Water.*

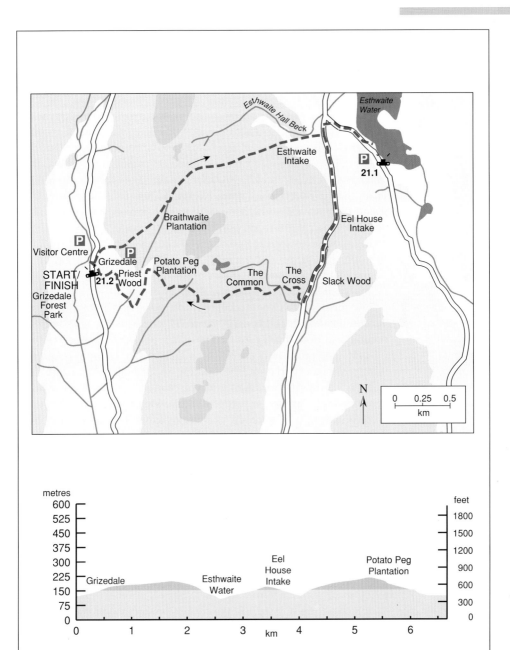

planned from the OLM. A northern loop taking in the Nab, or even venturing as far as Hawkshead, may interest more ambitious walkers.

WALK back to the road from the main carpark, turn R and within 100 paces, opposite the postbox, turn off acutely to the L to continue up the track marked 'Orienteering Start'. The marker post's coloured bands indicate (green) Silurian Way (15.2 km/9½ miles) and (white) Grizedale Tarn (5.2km/3¼ miles). From here, a rough, stony path winds moderately steeply uphill to the NE beneath a shading canopy of foliage provided by Douglas fir and European larch trees. You then pass the first of several interesting sculptures. Further up, there is a gap in the foliage on your R through which, in the clearest of conditions, it is possible to observe Blackpool Tower! At this point, be careful to avoid the public footpath leading through the gate on your R.

The most superb, tranquil views now open up to the S, revealing gentle, grassy hillocks liberally covered with a pleasing mixture of conifer and broadleaved trees. The steep gradient slackens further on and the track then connects with a wider forest road, along which you bear R to continue walking NE through a section of predominantly beech woodland. When you reach the T-junction a short distance further on turn L, still following the way indicated by a continuation of the green and white-banded marker posts. You then pass a fine group of sitka spruce growing on your L, which produce excellent timber. Further on, look out for a number of tiny secluded, bog pools, also off to your L.

When you reach the brow of the hill, there is a magnificent, open view over on your L, to the NE, of the distant high summits of Helvellyn, Fairfield and Red Screes, observed beyond another interesting sculpture in the foreground, this one depicting a fox carved from Furness sandstone. If the weather is clear here, turn around to locate Coniston Old Man rising behind you to the NW. Now comes a relatively tricky bit of route finding. Be careful to bear L at the next junction of ways and then follow the track around to the R, immediately avoiding turning off along the grassy path on your L which leads beneath power cables. The correct continuation way is now to the E.

Ahead there are sections of the track which often become muddy during wet weather and when forestry operations are being undertaken. The way then descends as you walk through Graythwaite Estates where the surrounding trees are mostly pine and spruce. The downwards slope steepens and when the track divides bear L, although this is not a critical manoeuvre as both branches merge further down the hillside.

166

Part of Esthwaite Water comes into view below on your L as you continue downhill, and a short distance further on, the track connects with a surfaced lane along which you turn L, still descending. This turning is at MR 357955. Opposite Esthwaite Cottage be vigilant to locate and follow a narrow path which is often overgrown. This leads off through dense foliage on the R. It is reached up a shallow bank and just ahead there is a concealed footpath sign which is not visible from the road. Cross over the P-stile, taking care to avoid the protruding barbed wire, and continue walking downhill to the E along a narrow, rarely used path through thick, invading bracken.

You will reach the lower road along the W shore of Esthwaite Water from Hawkshead at an electricity substation and you should turn R along this back lane. Be mindful of approaching traffic as you walk SE towards the lake, to arrive at Hawkshead Trout Farm. Go down to the lake here, where you can visit the farm shop and indulge in a spot of boating and fishing. After this, walk further SE along the beautiful lake shore, making use of a stile to cross a wire fence ahead. The views across Esthwaite Water, particularly on still, sunny days, are quite something, with pleasant, rolling green fellsides faithfully reflected on the becalmed surface of the lake. This delightful path soon reaches a secluded carparking area, where you may have to share the tranquillity of the surrounding landscapes with visitors who have walked no more than a few paces.

A short section of backtracking is now required. This is to return to the point at which you descended from the forested fellsides to reach the first surfaced lane. To do this, walk back up the adjacent road to pass by the trout farm again. Turn off L up the narrow, overgrown path when you reach the electricity substation and then turn L along the upper lane. Use this to return to the point to which you first descended from the forested area. On this occasion continue S, keeping to the surfaced lane, which leads uphill back into the forest. Continue walking along the lane for about 1.5 km (1 mile), studiously avoiding all forest tracks, including those protected by barriers, leading off to both L and R.

The way now undulates, before you need to turn off to the R at MR 355940½ along a signed public bridleway. Follow this around further to the R as it tracks uphill through a recently clear-felled section of the forest. This is towards 'The Cross' marked on the OLM. At the start the surface of the track is rough and stony but further up this changes to compacted earth divided by a central strip of grass. A fairly lengthy climb now follows, and the crossing of a small beck signifies that you are nearly at the top of the slope. The mature trees peter out when you reach the higher ground, the aftermath of previous harvesting operations.

A short distance further on your way connects with a wider forest road along which you bear R, soon walking westwards as this bends to the L. Then select the next waysigned footpath leading off on the L through an imposing wooden gate. This then leads through heather towards the brow of the fell. Turn around when you reach the top, weather permitting, to observe clear views of part of the Pennines far away to the E. In favourable conditions the Howgills, Crag Hill, Gragarth, Wernside and Ingleborough may all be spotted. The continuation path does get boggy in places as it tracks through areas that have been recently planted with a mixture of birch and spruce.

You continue to climb as the peaks of Coniston Old Man and Wetherlam reappear ahead on the R in the NW. The path then narrows appreciably, but the way always remains clear and obvious.

21.1 Boating on Esthwaite Water.

The occasional yellow waysign provides added confirmation that all is well. In fine weather, the most superb panorama of the complete Coniston Fells appears when you reach the highest point of the ridge. This includes, from s to n, the separate peaks of Brown and Buck Crags, Dow Crag, Coniston Old Man, Swirl How and Wetherlam.

From here the way is downhill along a clear path, which passes through a second high gate to reach a wide forest road. Cross this on a diagonal to your r, before bearing l along the waysigned and signposted track. This leads further down the slope in the shade of yet more tall trees. The way down steepens and, after a l turn down steps along a signed path, another forest road is reached. Turn l and

21.2 Grizedale Forest Park Centre and Shop.

s along this broad avenue, where you will pass some fine specimen Douglas fir trees with knobbly, fissured bark. Look out for Orienteering Post No 27 and, when you reach it, turn R to descend more steeply, following a clear path which incorporates another flight of steps.

When you reach marker post No 3 turn R again, continuing to walk downhill. Bear R again when you come to the next intersection of paths, to continue NW following a line of blue- and white-banded waysign posts.

Now be careful to keep to the higher path, avoiding a side track leading down on the L. The way you are following then passes close by a sculpture of a telescope pointing through a gap in the foliage on your L. Following this you cross an interesting long metal bridge spanning a deep, steep-sided gully. Over this watercourse there are more fascinating sculptures, including a group of axes and a herd of stags.

More wooden carvings and a monkey puzzle tree are passed before the way reaches an additional parking area serving the Forest Visitor Centre. Walk through this back to the road, turn R and the main features of the centre will be found down to the L, a short distance further on.

PLACES AND ACTIVITIES OF INTEREST

GRIZEDALE FOREST PARK

This is a superb outdoor venue manned by a team of dedicated forest rangers and other helpful staff. The Forest Visitor Centre is located about 4km (2½ miles) to the sw of Hawkshead at MR 336944 and there are large and convenient parking areas in the grounds.

The Visitor Centre is operated by Forest Enterprise at a small surplus, which is used to finance non-revenue amenities situated elsewhere in the Lake District. The Centre has become internationally famous for the 'Theatre in the Forest' and its forest sculptures. Grizedale offers a complete day in the great outdoors with a range of waymarked forest nature trails, adventure playground, picnic areas, forest shop, exhibition hall and tearoom. There are facilities for the disabled including 'Easirider' platforms which will enable those confined to wheelchairs to enjoy venturing into the forests in comfort and with easy manoeuvrability. *Guide maps and other information are available from the Centre (see Useful Addresses).*

THE GRIZEDALE SOCIETY

Since 1969 the Grizedale Society has developed and managed the 'Theatre in the Forest', the forest sculpture trails, sculpture gallery, craft workshop and painting studio.

The theatre is located in an expertly converted former coach house and hayloft, and international stars as well as local groups have performed before packed houses here. Best known as the host venue for the famous Grizedale International Piano Festival, the theatre offers a wide selection of events from opera to jazz and folk music, West End drama and multi-cultural dance.

Grizedale Forest contains the largest collection – over 70 exhibits – of site-specific sculpture in the United Kingdom. The main forest sculpture trail, The Silurian Way, is a healthy 15km (9½ miles) circular ramble passing sculptures from around the world The disabled are also catered for with The Ridding Wood Trail, a much shorter route which includes an aerial walkway and several musical sculptures. Parts of this trail have been redesigned to accommodate the 'Easiriders'. *Information on Grizedale Society events can be obtained from the Visitor Centre (see above).*

22 GUMMER'S HOW AND FELL FOOT PARK

STARTING/ FINISHING POINT
Forest Enterprise Gummer's How carpark. Pathfinder 626: MR 390876½.

GRADING OF WALK
Easy/ straightforward

TIME ALLOWANCE
1 hour

DISTANCE
1.6km (1 mile)

TOTAL HEIGHT GAINED
120m (395ft)

HIGHEST POINT
Gummer's How
321m (1055ft)

GRADIENTS

There is a gentle, uphill slope to the base of the steep, rocky pull to the summit of Gummer's How

PARKING

Gummer's How carpark holds 20–25 cars. Well screened in a forest clearing, it has picnic tables provided. There are also extensive parking facilities for cars and coaches at Fell Foot Park (Pathfinder 626: MR 382871)

PUBLIC TRANSPORT

Bus route 531 Kendal to Ambleside via Newby Bridge passes by Fell Foot Park (limited service)

GENERAL

The way to the summit of Gummer's How is along an obvious, well-drained path that leads to the base of the craggy summit, and then is followed by several alternative narrow ways up the rock face, where hand holds are occasionally necessary to steady yourself. Signs are in position but are hardly needed

TACKLING THE WALK

CASUAL WALKERS

This short walk involving an energetic climb should appeal to the vast majority of walkers, especially if you enjoy standing on the top of a fell with commanding views but you do not relish spending too much time or effort in getting there. There is more walking involved in exploring the lovely grounds of Fell Foot Park, and the combined distances should provide a flexible length to satisfy the needs of most walkers.

FAMILY WALKERS

The walk to the top of Gummer's Fell is already a well established and much-favoured family walk. Most children make it to the top without much trouble, and will not be too tired to enjoy themselves once they get there.

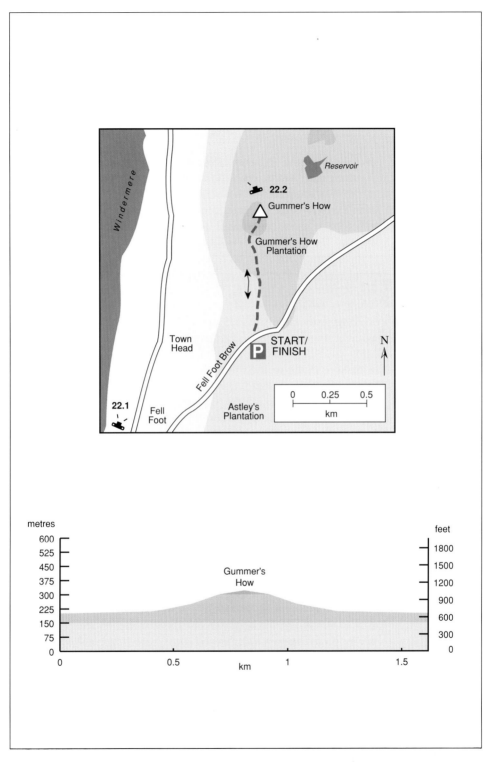

DEDICATED FELL WALKERS

The superb views to be observed from the summit of Gummer's How should provide an incentive for any walker. However, because there are restricted rights of way from the top of this isolated fell, it is not all that easy to plan extensions which might fully satisfy the demands of keen, energetic fell explorers. You could combine this walk with the following Walk 23.

START from the top end of the Gummer's How carpark walking along the broad track leading NE uphill through the trees. Almost immediately, branch L towards the road and cross this with care, passing through the two K-gates positioned on either side which allow convenient access through bordering dry stone walling. The path ahead is signed 'Public Footpath to Gummer's How Summit Only'. Before you go any further, look down to your L to admire the fine view over Lakeside and the southern tip of Windermere. On a fine day all is hustle and bustle down there with steamers, buses, trains and cars all converging on this popular spot. Snaking away from the end of the lake is the silver ribbon of the River Leven meandering through the Haverthwaite fells and woodlands. In clear weather the Coniston Fells may also be observed from here rising to the NW, with the separate peaks of Walna Scar, Brown Crag, Buck Crag, Dow Crag, Coniston Old Man and Swirl How silhouetted against the skyline. Further to the R the distinctive helmet shapes of the Langdale Pikes poke up, and between these two contrasting mountains the far-away, highest peaks of all, the Scafell Massif, put in an appearance when visibility is exceptionally good.

Directly ahead, and fortunately much closer to, is your main objective for today, the more modestly sized but nevertheless appealing, craggy summit of Gummer's How. This lies directly ahead to the N about 1km (½ mile) away. A gently rising, wide path comprised of a mixture of stones and compacted earth leads directly towards this peak, penetrating mixed woodlands of beech, hawthorn, larch, silver birch, spruce and sycamore to get there. The ground cover beneath this collection of trees is a mixture of bilberry, bracken, grasses and heathers. The undemanding, flatter section of the route leads quite quickly to rougher, steeper ground where progress up a refurbished stony path may be slow.

The way funnels up the steepening slopes in a series of twists and turns along a thoughtfully constructed and well-drained route. Further up, parts of the way resemble a gigantic staircase, with huge stone slabs providing the steps. This path provides a safe passage to the final craggy approach slopes to the summit area of Gummer's How, now in view a short distance above. The obvious way will lead you to the corner of a wire fence, positioned on your R. From this point, the continuation route to the top fans out into a number of narrower paths each providing a different angle of climb towards the top, and the most interesting ways up necessitating the occasional, steadying hand hold. The recommended ascent is up a middle course. This leads most directly ahead up a narrow, rough, stony path which rises steeply, twisting between craggy outcrops and loose rock debris.

All the routes to the top are well used and you should experience little difficulty in getting there, as time taken picking the best way ahead will inevitably slow you down to a comfortable rate of climb. The ascent is virtually complete when you spot the squarish summit cairn rearing up against the skyline above. The final approach to this cairn is easy, along a gently rising, grassy slope which forms the modest summit ridge of the fell. Although Gummer's How only commands a relatively modest elevation of 321m (1055ft) because it is an isolated fell situated at the s tip of Lakeland, it commands superb views in all directions, of which those N towards the heartland of the Lake District excel.

Many of the observations to be made from the summit of Gummer's How have already been located, but additional landscapes to be seen from here in good weather include Helvellyn and Fairfield to the N beyond Windermere, together with the long, folded ridges of the easterly fells, among which the peaks of Red Screes and High Street are dominant. Turning away from the attractions of

22.1 Fell Foot Park, Windermere and Gummer's How.

22.2 Windermere and the Lakeland Fells, observed from Gummer's How.

the Lake District, part of the backbone of England, the Pennines, stretches for several kilometres along the far E horizon. In clear weather the Howgills, Ingleborough, Pen-Y-Gent and Wernside can be identified rising here in the quadrant between ENE and ESE. In complete contrast, the flatness of Morecambe Bay with its glistening sands, mud banks and water channels stretches away as far as the eye can see to the S.

Before you retrace your steps back to the carpark, explore the summit area a little more thoroughly. Start by walking a short distance further N along the grassy sward to be rewarded by a more complete view of the entire length of Windermere far below. Also make your way to the W rim of the summit crag to absorb a complete exposure of Lakeside and the attractive, densely wooded shores converging on the southern tip of Windermere to squeeze the lake into the River Leven. From here, on your far L and to the SW you can make out part of the Duddon Valley and its estuary spilling into Morecambe Bay.

When you have seen enough, make your way back to the carpark. As a further alternative to the series of paths you observed during the ascent, there is a grassy path leading eastwards from the summit area which circles back to connect with your approach path lower down.

PLACES AND ACTIVITIES OF INTEREST

FELL FOOT PARK AND GARDEN

Fell Foot Park and Garden, owned and administered by the National Trust, occupies 18 acres of outstandingly beautiful lakeshore parkland situated at the southern end of Windermere. There are ample parking facilities for cars and coaches and the Park offers picnic areas, an adventure playground, boating and fishing, and walkabouts. There is an information centre and gift shop and a boat-house café in which exhibitions are displayed. There is access to these for the disabled, including the use of a two-seater buggy vehicle.

The park is currently undergoing exciting changes in that the Trust is conserving and enhancing what was a typical late Victorian garden of rhododendrons, oaks and pines. These originally framed a bow-fronted house owned by the late Colonel Ridehalgh, which was sadly demolished in 1907. A major aspect of the restoration work is to reclaim the original views across the site and down to the lake. These ambitious refurbishment plans also include the replacement of paths shown on the 1890 and 1913 OS maps, restoring the original basic figure of eight around the Park, and the introduction of Victorian-style seating concentrated on the old house lawn.

For further information contact Fell Foot Park and Garden (see Useful Addresses).

One of the most satisfying views in the whole of southern Lakeland happens to be from the lakeside at the Park. This is NE towards the summit of Gummer's How, and is particularly rewarding when you consider that you have just been up there!

23 LAKESIDE & HAVERTHWAITE RAILWAY, BIGLAND TARN AND FINSTHWAITE

STARTING/ FINISHING POINT
Lakeside station.
Pathfinder map
626: MR 377874.
The walk starts from
Haverthwaite station (MR 349½842)
and finishes at
Lakeside station

GRADING OF WALK
Moderate/
challenging

TIME ALLOWANCE
4 hours

DISTANCE
10km (6.2 miles)

TOTAL HEIGHT GAINED
210m (690ft)

HIGHEST POINT
Hard Crag
160m (525ft)

GRADIENTS

There are two quite severe uphill sections, the first up through Birk Dault Wood to reach Bigland Tarn and the other towards the end of the walk, to pass through Wintering Park

PARKING

Massive parking facilities at the train and boat terminus, but these are extremely popular and fill up quickly. There is also a café and toilets

PUBLIC TRANSPORT

Bus route 518 Barrow to Ambleside passes through nearby Newby Bridge

GENERAL

The paths are good and clear for most of the way, but not across Bigland Barrow. Route signing is also variable

TACKLING THE WALK

CASUAL WALKERS

This route will be a challenging one for the majority of less energetic walkers, and in places route finding is not all that obvious. One suggestion is to walk as far as Bigland Tarn and, if you feel confident from there, continue to Newby Bridge where, if need be, you can short-circuit the final loop through Finsthwaite by walking up the road, which will take you directly back to Lakeside.

FAMILY WALKERS

The full walk will almost certainly be too strenuous for families other than those with sturdy teenagers. Families with younger children should either walk to Bigland Tarn and then retrace their steps, or catch a return train and alight at Newby Bridge Halt, completing the short loop N through Finsthwaite.

178

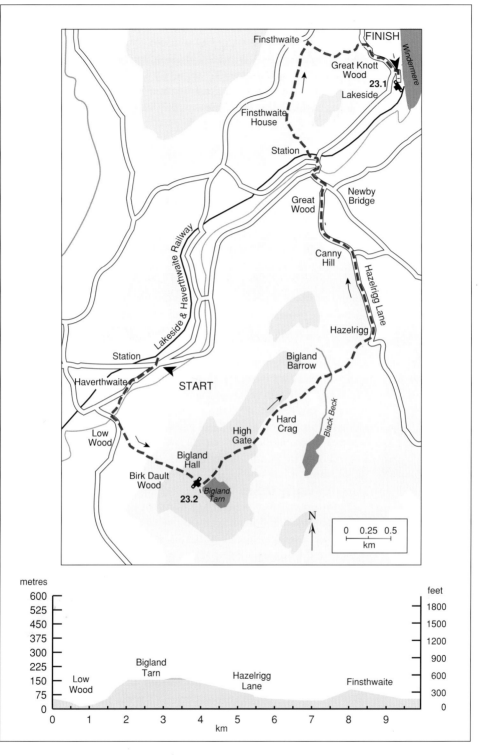

Finsthwaite

FINISH

Great Knott
Wood

23.1

Lakeside

Windermere

Finsthwaite
House

Station

Newby
Bridge

Great
Wood

Canny
Hill

Hazelrigg Lane

Lakeside & Haverthwaite Railway

Hazelrigg

Station

Bigland
Barrow

Haverthwaite

START

Low
Wood

High
Gate

Hard
Crag

Black Beck

Bigland
Hall

Birk Dault
Wood

23.2

Bigland
Tarn

N

| 0 | 0.25 | 0.5 |
| km |

metres
feet

600 — 1800
525 —
450 — 1500
375 — 1200
300 —
225 — 900

Bigland
Tarn

Hazelrigg
Lane

150 — 600
Low
Wood

Finsthwaite

75 — 300

0 — 0

0   1   2   3   4   5   6   7   8   9
km

DEDICATED FELL WALKERS

This walk at the s end of Lakeland may take you into an area which is new to you and for this reason alone is well worth considering. The route described is full of interest and if you incorporate the train journey as suggested it will occupy most of the day. There are opportunities for extending the walk if you desire, but with route finding in places presenting a challenge, and much to see and absorb, it is doubtful whether – in view of the time contraints – this will be possible.

AREFUL planning will be needed to fit this walk in with the scheduled trian timetable, particularly if you aim to complete the entire route, in which case you may need to catch the earliest possible train from Lakeside. Situated at the southern tip of Windermere lakeside, this is a splendid starting location. Steamers ply to and fro along the lake, the jetties are crammed with colourful sailing craft at rest, the comfortable Lakeside Hotel will cater for your refreshment needs on its relaxing lawns, and the views across and up the length of Windermere on a beautiful, sunny morning are fantastic. The obvious advice is get there well before your train is due to leave.

The train journey to Haverthwaite takes less than 20 minutes and you will find that this passes very quickly indeed, as there is a great deal to observe along the way by the wooded banks of the River Leven. The train soon reaches Newby Bridge Halt; take note of this stop, which you might wish to use for part of your return journey. The engine puffs off again, now along a wooded valley hemmed in by gentle, rounded fells, and in what seems like very little time at all the train is slowing down as it pulls into Haverthwaite terminus.

From the railway station, walk across the busy A590 (T) road, exercising care and making good use of the island sanctuary separating the two carriageways at this spot. Then turn off along the minor road leading sw and continue down the footpath adjacent to the R side of this lane. The way passes by a memorial in the form of a huge stone cross and after this keep L of the Angler's Arms, walking downhill. At the approach to a huddle of buildings ahead (timber merchants) veer L down the side lane, to follow the way directed by yellow waymarkers through the yard and between the buildings. Bear L again to leave through a K-gate at the far end of the yard. This provides access to a continuation footpath.

The path now bends around further to the L beside a line of trees which fringe the River Leven, flowing placidly below. Your direction is now to the sw. Turn L when you reach the road ahead, having successfully negotiated your way across a patch of approach

180

23.1 Steaming into Lakeside.

ground that is often muddy. Cross over the Leven by the attractive arched bridge and walk straight past the first side lane to your L which is signed to Bigland Hall, continuing down the road signed to Holker 4½. A short distance beyond a second turning off on the L, select a waysigned footpath also on the L. This is part of the signed Cumbria Coastal Way. The entrance to this path is positioned on a particularly dangerous bend in the road so, do be careful here, especially if you have young children in your care.

A wide path now leads gently uphill through Birk Dault Wood, a splendid mixture of ash, beech, birch, hazel, Scots pine and sycamore, with a liberal covering of bracken underneath. Woodland birds flutter about among the foliage, which is obviously much to their liking. Keep to the main path as it forks R up a brow ahead, weaving through the woodland. Higher up, keep following the obvious continuation track as this leads you across an open patch of ground, before crossing a cart track and entering more woodland beneath a group of feathery larch trees. The gradient now steepens appreciably, but the reward for this increased effort is the superb views of the wide, wooded valley of the meandering River Leven, now far below, which appear to your rear.

The way passes by a confirmatory yellow marker post as it continues eastwards still gaining height. Along here, be careful to avoid a side track leading off to the R. Scurrying grouse in large numbers may be observed in the vicinity. The climb is quite demanding and leads eventually to a wooden gate, where another waysign has been helpfully positioned on a dry stone wall. This marks the entry into more open countryside, and this is revealed progressively as you continue up a less demanding slope ahead. A path of stone and grass winds further up the fellside through the few remaining trees and then fringes a track on the R, before veering off to the L to edge by another waysigned post. Then, over the next brow, the cool, clear waters of Bigland Tarn will focus your attention ahead. This tarn occupies a truly tranquil setting and the peace of this oasis, surrounded by gentle, rounded fellsides, is not disturbed by either the antics of waterfowl or the sounds of anglers contentedly casting their lines. Time to take a rest.

To round the north-western part of the tarn, bear L and pass through the waysigned K-gate to walk to the northern tip of the water. Then follow the wide shale track as it bends to the L away from the tarn and also away from a stile there, restricted to use by fee-paying anglers and signed 'No Public Access'. The track heads NE to reach a lane and private carparking area serving those with fishing permits. This is named as High Gate on the Pathfinder map and is located at MR 360833½. Bear R here to pass through the two K-gates provided for the purpose of avoiding a cattle grid. On a clear day there are fine views to your L along here as you walk down the fenced and surfaced lane ahead. These include sightings of Helvellyn, Fairfield, Red Screes and the Ill Bell spur far away towards N.

Through a metal gate, the way leads gently uphill beneath trees. Through gaps in these, the Coniston Fells may be observed to the NW, with the peaks of Dow Crag and Coniston Old Man and the easternmost of the craggy spurs of sprawling Wetherlam discernible. Pass through the imposing stone gateway to reach another lane, which you cross before proceeding along the public footpath leading off opposite. This is signed to Hazelrigg and is reached through a wooden gate, positioned to the R of the sign. A grassy track leads NE from here, passing above a fenced-off area of machinery. The way then passes by another wooded area, this one down to your R, before it climbs up the brow ahead, passing through the remains of a dilapidated stone wall in the process. Ignore the side path down to the R along here.

The route then penetrates more craggy, higher ground with abundant outcrops of rock. There are more superb views in all directions from these heights, and further on the irregular shape of the artificial lake from which Black Beck flows may be observed down to your R. This serves as a trout fishery. After this, your grassy way begins to drop downhill, and at the junction ahead ignore the grassy side path leading off uphill through an inviting gateway. Your better-defined way continues to track NE to reach another gateway, where there is a concentration of converging ways. Continue ahead along the grassy path in the direction which may be arrowed 'EHPS' (Endurance Horse and Pony Society), still continuing gently downhill and walking through clumps of juntas grass and prickly gorse bushes.

Route finding from here becomes a little more exacting, and in one place quite exasperating. For the time being, continue predominantly downhill to the NE following the narrow but mostly clearly defined path, crossing over a small beck and then climbing up a shallow brow in the process. Ignore several branch paths in tracking NE along what is invariably the better-defined way. This leads for some distance to the L of a dry stone wall up a relatively rough section of a stony path. The route then kinks temporarily to your L, scaling higher ground and skirting Bigland Barrow. Be careful when you reach the next intersection of ways, as some of these are used for horse trails and on occasions are marked with bright orange tape which can be confusing.

Now be careful to avoid a wide track leading further uphill as this goes to Backbarrow, which is not on your route. Instead, proceed with confidence through the gap ahead and then veer L along a narrow path, ignoring a wider way to your R. Your path becomes less distinct but persevere, keeping to the higher ground and walking through the pervading bracken. Continue walking ENE, traversing down a craggy slope, and then make directly towards the wall ahead to your L. Follow this down, walking about 20 paces to the R of it along a faintly discernible path. This leads to a narrow and important route-finding gap in the stone wall near to its corner. Turn L to pass through this. Continue further downhill maintaining your ENE bearing to reach and pass through a metal gate. Turn immediately R after this, to descend through conifers to the lane below. (It is possible that this section of your route may have been improved and made easier to follow by the time you are walking through.)

Turn L along the lane, walking NE away from the nearby cattle grid. The route connects with the approach lane to Hazelrigg Farm, off to your R. Bear L along this approach lane to head NNW. Avoid the temptation to use any of the footpaths leading off to your R and signed to Newby Bridge, as these involve further complications and do become very muddy in wet conditions. Instead march along the narrow, quiet lane to pass by Harebridge House and then ignore the footpath on the L, which leads to Backbarrow. The shaded lane leads downhill where a side lane and another footpath both off to the R should be avoided as you continue walking down directly towards Newby Bridge.

The lane leads to the busy A590 (T) road at Lakes End B&B guest house. Cross over with care and turn L along the pavement after

crossing the adjacent wide grass verge. Then turn off R towards
Lakeside, to cross over the River Leven by the road bridge, where
there is no protective footpath over the narrow arch. Follow the
road as it bends L away from the Swan Hotel, with its riverside tea
terrace that may prove irresistible! In continuing, be careful to walk
past a turning on the L signed to Finsthwaite and Rusland. Walk up
the brow ahead, keeping to the road, and use this to cross the railway line. Then turn immediately L along a track signed 'Private
Road – No Parking'. This doubles as a public footpath.

The path initially leads westward, before bending R towards NW
where it is signed 'Footpath Finsthwaite'. Resist climbing over a
stile on your R here. The correct way leads uphill again, to a
waysigned stile adjacent to a wooden gate. The woodlands of
Wintering Park are entered at this point, and further uphill you

need to branch L as directed by another waysign. There are more steep slopes ahead, these through mixed deciduous woodland consisting of beech, birch, holly, oak and sycamore, with plenty of bracken once again growing in their shade. The clear, obvious path brings you to more open meadowlands, which are accessed over a s-stile which breaches a stone wall. A yellow waysign is in position here.

The way continues northwards through a gap in the surrounding woodland and across lush grasslands, where all you have to do is to keep to the path indicated by more waysigns. Various stiles are used as the continuation way leads through stretches that are prone to becoming wet. Keep walking northwards using a white-painted building ahead as a marker, and this direction will lead you to an iron K-gate positioned directly opposite St Peter's Church at

23.2 A sunny day at Bigland Tarn.

Finsthwaite. This is a splendidly proportioned building and there are seats provided in the perimeter walling which might tempt you into stopping for a rest.

Turn R and SE along the walled lane to pass the school house built in 1874. A gate then provides access to more pleasant green fields leading slightly uphill. Pass through a gap in a stone wall to continue SE across sloping meadows and reach an S-stile in the stone wall ahead. This provides an entrance to Great Knott Wood, where an ancient seat is located. Bear immediately L to continue along the clearly defined, wide path which winds NE to connect with the road again a short distance further on. This is opposite a residence interestingly named Buck Yeats North. Turn R and follow the road the short distance back to Lakeside, turning L when you reach the Lakeside Hotel to collect your vehicle.

PLACES AND ACTIVITIES OF INTEREST

THE LAKESIDE AND HAVERTHWAITE RAILWAY

The track of this railway was formally part of the Furness Railway Branch Line, which carried passengers and freight from Ulverston to Lakeside. The only part now remaining is the 5.5km (3½ miles) stretch from Haverthwaite through Newby Bridge to the terminus at Lakeside. Here, connections may be made with the boats which ply the length of Windermere, stopping at Bowness or Ambleside (through tickets for this combined excursion are available).

The Furness Railway was developed in the 1850s and 60s at the height of the Industrial Revolution, when its principal business was the transportation of bulk iron ore and coal. It later became an important passenger line. Since then it has had a colourful history, but with a progressive decline in usage the branch line to Lakeside suffered closure to passenger traffic in 1965, and the restricted freight service was finally terminated on 2 April 1967. The current operating company provides a booklet summarizing the fascinating story of how the line was saved, to be reopened partially on 2 May 1973.

For further information and a timetable, contact the Lakeside & Haverthwaite Railway Co Ltd (see Useful Addresses).

BIGLAND TARN

This is a quite superbly located natural stretch of water trapped between low, wooded fells and dammed by glacial debris. It is fed by several springs and its outlet stream feeds the River Leven some distance below. The tarn is popular for coarse fishing and is well frequented by pairs of mating swans and many other waterfowl. Sedge, rush and other marginal plants fringe its shallow waters, and these provide shelter and nesting spots for its varied birdlife.

USEFUL ADDRESSES

BRANTWOOD
Coniston
Cumbria LA21 8AD
Tel: 015394 41396

Jumping Jenny Tearooms
Tel: 015394 41715

BROWNS MOTORS AND COACHES
Market Place, Ambleside
Cumbria LA22 9BU
Tel: 015394 2205

CUMBRIA TOURIST BOARD
Ashleigh
Holly Road, Windermere
Cumbria LA23 2AQ
Tel: 015394 44444

ENGLISH HERITAGE
North Regional Office
Bessie Surtees House
41 Sandhill
Newcastle-upon-Tyne NE1 3JF
TEL: 0191 2611585

ESKDALE MILL
Boot Village, Holme Park
Cumbria CA19 1TG
Tel: 019467 23335

FELL FOOT PARK AND GARDEN
Newby Bridge, Ulverston
Cumbria LA21 8NN
Tel: 015395 31273

GRIZEDALE FOREST PARK VISITOR CENTRE
Hawkshead, Ambleside
Cumbria LA22 0QJ
Tel: 01229 860010

KESWICK ON DERWENTWATER LAUNCH CO LTD
c/o 29 Manor Park, Keswick
Cumbria CA12 4AB
Tel: 017687 72263

LAKE DISTRICT NATIONAL PARK

LAKE DISTRICT NATIONAL PARK AUTHORITY
Murley Moss
Oxenholme Road, Kendal
Cumbria LA9 7RL
Tel: 01539 724555
(Administration and Planning)

THE BLENCATHRA CENTRE
Threlkeld, Keswick
Cumbria
Tel: 017687 79601
(Park Management Field Studies
Council/NPA Study Centre)

BROCKHOLE VISITOR CENTRE
Windermere
Cumbria LA23 1JL
Tel: 015394 46601
(Park Management and Visitor
Services)

TOURIST INFORMATION CENTRES

Bowness Bay	Tel: 015394 42895
Coniston	Tel: 015394 41533
Grasmere	Tel: 015394 35245
Hawkshead	Tel: 015394 86525
Keswick	Tel: 017687 72803
Pooley Bridge	Tel: 017684 86530
Seatoller Barn	Tel: 017687 77294
Ullswater	Tel: 017684 82414
Waterhead	Tel: 015394 32729

WEATHER LINE
Tel: 017687 75757 (24 hours)

LAKESIDE & HAVERTHWAITE RAILWAY CO LTD
Haverthwaite Station
Nr Ulverston
Cumbria LA12 8AL
Tel: 015395 31954

MOUNTAIN GOAT (MINIBUSES)
Victoria Street, Windermere
Cumbria LA23 1AD
Tel: 015394 45161

MUNCASTER CASTLE
Ravenglass
Cumbria CA18 1RQ
Tel: 01229 717614/717203 (Office)
      01229 717203 (Castle)
      01229 717311 (Gate)
      01229 717393 (Owl Centre)

NATIONAL TRUST
The Hollens
Grasmere, Ambleside
Cumbria LA22 9QZ
Tel: 015394 35599

NATIONAL TRUST (ENTERPRISES) LTD
Gondola Bookings
Pier Cottage, Coniston
Cumbria LA21 8AJ
Tel: 015394 41288

NORTH WEST WATER AUTHORITY
Mintsfeet Road South, Kendal
Cumbria LA9 4BY
Tel: 01539 740066

RAVENGLASS & ESKDALE RAILWAY CO LTD
Ravenglass
Cumbria CA18 1SW
Tel: 01229 717171

STAGECOACH (CUMBERLAND)
Tangier Street, Whitehaven
Cumbria CA28 7XF
Tel: 01946 63222 (Bus
Information)
Tel: 01946 592000 (Head Office)

TELETOURIST EVENT LINE
Tel: 015394 46363

ULLSWATER NAVIGATION AND TRANSIT CO LTD
13 Maude Street, Kendal
Cumbria LA9 4QD
Tel: 01539 721626
Or   Pier House, Glenridding
Tel: 017684 82229

WHINLATTER FOREST PARK VISITOR CENTRE
Forest Enterprise
Braithwaite, Keswick
Cumbria CA12 5TW
Tel: 017687 78469

YMCA
National Centre
Lakeside, Ulverston
Cumbria LA1Z 8BD
Tel: 015395 31758

YOUTH HOSTELS ASSOCIATION
Central Regional Office
PO Box 11, Matlock
Derbyshire DE4 2XA
Tel: 01629 825850

CONTACT TELEPHONE NUMBERS

CONISTON LAUNCH
Tel: 015394 36216

DOVE COTTAGE AND WORDSWORTH MUSEUM
Tel: 015394 35544/35547

KIRKSTONE GALLERIES
Tel: 015394 34002

RYDAL MOUNT
Tel: 015394 33002

PLATTY (CANOES – DERWENT WATER)
Tel: 017687 77282

STAKIS KESWICK LODORE
Tel: 017687 77285

MOUNTAIN RESCUE SERVICE
999 EMERGENCY

GLOSSARY

The following geological terms and dialect words have been used in the book or may be met with by those undertaking the walks.

arête a sharp, pointed ridge
beck stream
bield sheltered or protected land
cairn heap of stones, typically conical, used as a position indicator
col sharp-edged or saddle-shaped pass
crag steep, rugged rock or peak
culvert drain or covered channel
dale valley
dub pool
edge steep cliff
fault fracture in rocks, the opposite sides of which have been displaced relative to one another, vertically or horizontally
fell hill or mountain
force waterfall
ghyll/gill watercourse, usually in a ravine
gorge deep, narrow, steep-walled valley
hause summit of a narrow pass or col
how rounded hill
knoll small, rounded hill
knott rocky outcrop
limestone sedimentary rock composed almost entirely of calcium carbonate, mainly as calcite
nab/neb promontory
pike pointed summit
rigg ridge
sandstone sedimentary rock of sand and/or silt bound together by a cement, often calcite or silica. Quartz grains predominate in the average sandstone
scar escarpment
scree loose, shattered rock on a mountain slope
shale fine-grained sedimentary rock formed predominantly of compacted clay
squeezer stile stile containing a narrow gap
tarn small expanse of water
thwaite clearing
tor core of unweathered, harder rocks standing above a surrounding area of weathered rock

SUMMARY TABLE

WALK	DESCRIPTION	GRADING OF WALK		WALKING TIME	DISTANCE (EXCLUDING HEIGHT)		TOTAL HEIGHT GAINED		HIGHEST POINT	
		EASY/ STRAIGHTFORWARD	MODERATE/ CHALLENGING	HOURS	KM	MILES	METRES	FEET	METRES	FEET
KESWICK, BORROWDALE AND THE NORTHERN FELLS										
1	Whinlatter Forest Park, Barf and Lord's Seat	*		4	7.3	4.5	250	820	552	1810
2	Castlerigg Stone Circle and St John's in the Vale Church	*		3	6.4	4	180	590	260	855
3	Boat Trips on Derwent Water and Lakeside Walk to Lodore Falls	*		2	4.6	2.9	20	65	60	195
THE WESTERN DALES AND FELLS										
4	Around Buttermere	*		2½	7	4.4	45	150	120	395
5	Around Ennerdale Water		*	4½	12.5	7.8	30	100	130	425
6	Wasdale Head and Styhead Tarn		*	4	8.4	5.2	460	1510	495	1625
7	Ravenglass & Eskdale Railway and Muncaster Fell	*	*	3	7.3	4.5	250	820	231	760
THE LANGDALE VALLEYS										
8	Around Blea Tarn	*		1½	2.2	1.4	45	150	213	700
9	Elterwater, Skelwith Force, Colwith Force and Slater Bridge	*	*	3½	8.9	5.6	155	510	150	490
10	Loughrigg Tarn and Skelwith Force	*		1½	3.2	2	45	150	105	345
AROUND GRASMERE AND AMBLESIDE										
11	Grasmere, Rydal Water and Wordsworth	*		3	9.9	6.1	60	195	120	395
12	Silver How and Rowing Boats		*	3	5.8	3.6	305	1000	394	1295
13	Alcock Tarn and Wordsworth		*	3	4.5	2.8	340	1115	375	1230
14	Stockghyll Force, Wansfell Pike and Jenkin Crag		*	3½	6.2	3.8	450	1475	484	1590
PATTERDALE, GLENRIDDING AND ULLSWATER										
15	Boat Trip on Ullswater and Lakeside Walk from Howtown	*		4	10.5	6.5	245	805	210	690
16	Aira Force, Dockray and Common Fell		*	3½	7	4.2	390	1280	553	1815
17	Hartsop and Brothers Water		*	1½	4.5	2.8	35	115	185	605
AROUND CONISTON										
18	Tarn Hows and Black Crag	*		2½	6.7	4.2	170	560	322	1055
19	Gondola, Brantwood and Crag Head	**	*	1½	2.1	1.3	140	460	230	755
20	Torver Back Common, Coniston Water and Mill Bridge	**		3	5.8	3.6	205	670	150	490
SOUTHERN LAKELAND										
21	Grizedale Forest Park and Esthwaite Water	*		3	6.7	4.2	225	735	210	690
22	Gummer's How and Fell Foot Park	*	*	1	1.6	1	120	395	321	1055
23	Lakeside & Haverthwaite Railway, Bigland Tarn and Finsthwaite	*		4	10	6.2	210	690	160	525

INDEX

Page numbers in *italic* refer to the photographs.